100 Years

of

Scouting in Connah's Quay

Sue Copp

1st Connah's Quay Scout
Centenary Project

100 Years of Scouting in Connah's Quay
first published in Wales in 2007
on behalf of the 1st Connah's Quay Scouts
by
BRIDGE BOOKS
61 Park Avenue
Wrexham
Ll12 7AW

Supported by the
Heritage Lottery Fund

ISBN 978-1-84494-036-3

A CIP entry for this book is available from the British Library

Printed and bound by
CROMWELL PRESS LTD
Trowbridge, Wiltshire

This book is dedictaed
to
Allan Roberts, who kept the B-P spirit
going in Connah's Quay into the 21st century

As the flames leap upwards
So be our aims
As the red log glows
So be our sympathies
As the grey ash fades
So be our errors
As the good campfire warms the circle
So may our ideals warm the world
Brother Scouts, the campfire is open

Campfire,
Welsh Jamboree at Picton Castle,
Haverfordwest, 1952.

Acknowledgements

The Centenary Project has been supported with funding from the Heritage Lottery Fund. This book has been compiled by 1st Connah's Quay Scout Explorer Scouts and the Centenary Committee in partnership with Flintshire Historical Society.

Explorer Scouts: Jamie Duncan, Paul Griffiths, Ben Hall, Ben Hicks, Ian Letley, Terry Owen, Richard Roberts, Matthew Styles, Andrew Wallis and Owen Wynne.

Centenary Committee: Sue Copp, Ron Jones, Colin Leonard, Joan Oldfield, John & Norma Parker, Ken Taylor, Geoffrey Veysey, Vic Williams & Pat Wilson.

Text: Sue Copp.

Contributions from: Brian Jones, David Williams, Ian Matthews, Tessa Christian, Ann McFerran, Christine Roberts, Dave Rowlands, Arthur Jones and Raymond Gregory.

Proof reading and editing: Geoffrey Veysey.

Research: Vic Williams, Sue Copp, Harvey Lloyd.

Oral History: Ken Howarth, Paul Griffiths, Andrew Wallis, Richard Roberts, Jamie Duncan, Ian Letley, Ben Hicks, Ken Taylor, Joan Oldfield, Ron Jones, Roy Christian.

Interviews from: Glyn Barham, Gilbert Butler, John Butler, Alan Henshaw, Gordon Henshaw, Allan Roberts, Blodwen Roberts, Dave Rowlands, Norman Scattergood, Mark Sephton and Ken Taylor.

Heritage Trail: Debbie Snow, Richard Roberts, Paul Griffiths, Jamie Duncan and Owen Wynne.

Photographs: Ken Howarth, Richard Roberts, Ron Jones, Joan Oldfield, Sue Copp.

The Centenary Committee also extends its thanks to the Flintshire Record Office, Flintshire County Library and the Museum Service and to the following individuals and organisations for their help and support during this project:

Rev. Paul Varah, Vicar of St. Mark's Church; Bengal Dynasty Restaurant; Brown's Furniture Warehouse; British Nuclear Fuels; Carl Sargeant, AM; Cllr Freda Macdonald, Gary Feather (Town Clerk) and the staff of Connah's Quay Town Council; Dave Rowlands; Harvey Lloyd; Raymond Gregory; Castle Cement; Deeside College; I*D Books; Hawarden Camera Club; Jimsul Construction; Lord Barry Jones; Toyota UK Ltd; Marc Tami, MP; Warwick International; The Scout Association at Gilwell Park; Professor Dave Loades, Welsh Scout Council.

Thanks also to all the people who gave permission for their photographs to be used in this book: Gilbert Butler, Ken Taylor, Harvey Lloyd, Roy and Tessa Christian, Allan and Christine Roberts, Ron Jones and Norman Scattergood. Other photographs have been reproduced courtesy of Mrs M. E Coppack, Graham Catherall and Corus. The postcards of old Connah's Quay are in the archives of the Flintshire Record Office. Despite every effort, we have been unable to discover who produced them.

Finally, a special thanks to Dr Kathryn Ellis and Steve Roberts at the History Department at NEWI for inspiring a fascination for the history of north-east Wales and without whom this book would not have been written.

Foreword

by

Chief Scout Peter Duncan

I send you all my best wishes as you read this book produced by the 1st Connah's Quay Scouts Centenary Project.

Our Movement has come a long way since Baden-Powell had the inspiration to direct us to the wider Scouting Trail. We are blessed with innumerable benefits when we join Scouting. Not least amongst these are the friends we make and the experiences we share. I am delighted that so many individuals will be sharing their personal reminiscences with you in this centenary book. Their stories give a terrific flavour of the first 100 successful years of Scouting tradition in Connah's Quay.

With my very best wishes for the future as you bring the magic of Scouting to new generations of young people in Connah's Quay.

Message

from

May Castrey

District Commissioner, Flintshire District

Congratulations 1st Connah's Quay Group!

It's not very often that a group celebrates 100 years of continuous service, and I'm delighted to have such a Group in Flintshire District, and with such a distinguished record.

You have ridden all the changes in uniform and programme that Scouting has seen in its lifetime. The spirit which B-P encouraged is still with you, and long may it continue. This is a very exciting and memorable way in which to celebrate your centenary. So many people have contributed to the history and achievements of Connah's Quay Group. My own small claim to fame is that I made some tea, and laid a few bricks during the construction of the present building, back in the early 1960s, and I stole a Leader for my husband. The success of the Group can be attributed to the loyalty and dedication of the Leaders and Supporters, some of whom have given a lifetime of service to Scouting. I salute them all.

May the Group continue to flourish and have further successes in the next 100 years.

Message

from

Gilbert Butler

It was 1934/35 when I first joined the 'TROOP' as it was then called, under the leadership of my very first Scoutmaster, Lt.-Com. E. Ll. Marriott, RNR, and Mr Stretch, the Assistant Scoutmaster.

Little did I realise that some seventy-one years on I would be writing a short message for this book which highlights the role that the Group played in the history of Connah's Quay in its one hundred years of existence.

The most pleasing thought is that in all those years the Group has not closed, and has offered Scouting to the community.

The Group has always been well looked after by a succession of GOOD quality Leaders, who incidentally, came up through the ranks, as it were, and have always maintained the Tradition of Scouting that many still remember.

During my lifetime as a member of the Group I have made many friends and I still meet up with them occasionally. We discuss the happy events, camps and the days in the Old Tin Hut on the Brickfield site to the present HQ on Tuscan Way.

I have always been proud to be a member of the Group and hopefully I will be able to support Scouting in Connah's Quay for some considerable time.

I must congratulate everyone, the Young People of the Group, parents who support the Group Committee members and also the Leaders of the Group who give and have given their time to maintain the high quality of Scouting in Connah's Quay.

May the group go from strength to strength in the future.

Thank you for allowing me to write this short contribution to your book.

Introduction

by

Sir William Gladstone, K.G.

This is a wonderful book. Although it is quite short, it tells you more about Scouting over the course of a hundred years than any long and weighty official history could do. It is made up mainly of the experiences of many of the individual people who have been involved, skilfully woven together.

Above all we can glimpse the enjoyment so many boys have had from Scouting over all these years, from camping in farmers' fields with their trek carts to expending their surplus energy on games in the Scout Hut. We can see how Scouting has changed over the years to suit the needs of each new generation.

We read about the help and support so many people have given to Scouting in Connah's Quay: the Scoutmasters of the early years, the Leaders and helpers of today, each bringing to Scouting their own particular contribution. Huge amounts of hard work are contributed free of charge – because of the happiness and satisfaction people feel from working in a team to support such a splendid activity as Scouting.

Each period brings its opportunities and its problems. Over the course of a century there have been ups and downs (but as far more ups than downs). We read about them as they come – just as they do in all of our lives. We see how the opportunities are grasped, and how the challenges are met, by groups of people putting their heads together and contributing their resources – above all their time. We don't have to analyse why Scouting is so worthwhile; we can get the feel of it through the eyes and ears of all the people mentioned in the book.

Some of the people we read about are outstanding. They have made huge individual contributions. This book pays tribute to them simply by describing what they did from week to week and from year to year. A very important feature of Scouting is the Scouting Family, involving several generations; Connah's Quay has been fortunate in its Scouting Families. This is not surprising for those of us who are familiar with The Quay's remarkable character and enterprise. It takes its place amongst a few very special villages (now the size of quite big towns, if the truth be admitted) which began as small settlements in north-east Wales and which have grown and developed into truly remarkable places. You find enterprising and original people who have been born and bred there far afield, throughout Britain and the wider world.

What is it that has made The Quay such a special place? Well its Scouting has certainly contributed.

The 1st Connah's Quay Scout Group has every reason to be proud of its record as one of the very first groups to be founded. It is to be congratulated on its enterprise in publishing this history as a major part of its celebration of the centenary of Scouting It is important that we understand our past. It is where we came from. It has made us what we are, and it can give us an idea of what we might be.

Preface

by

Sue Copp

Connah's Quay Scouts Dig Deep for their Roots
(Connah's Quay Scouts Centenary Project)

This project started in 2004 with a desire to celebrate the fact that we were nearly one hundred years old. It began with an attempt to collect artefacts and memorabilia and stage an exhibition but the idea evolved into something altogether more ambitious!

Our centenary committee found out about a marvellous opportunity to really dig deep for our roots with the help of a Heritage Lottery Grant called 'Young Roots' and, in October 2005, our dream was realised with a generous grant from this fund. In order to qualify we had to have a partner organisation to provide historical expertise and we could not have found a better one than the Flintshire Historical Society. We also had the support of lots of local firms and organisations who loved our plan. It is a fact that many who have shown their goodwill and generosity have had some connection with scouts; either personally or through their fathers or grandfathers ... there cannot be many families living in Connah's Quay who have not been affected by scouting. Equally, there are some families who have, in turn, profoundly affected scouts. In the pages of this book you will notice that there are certain families who all seem to belong to the group in some capacity from one generation to the next ... cub, scout, explorer, scouter, parents' committee. These are people whose tireless efforts have ensured the survival of the group throughout the century. The scout group remained open through two world wars, played its part in the home front and survived the depression.

Connah's Quay Scouts Group started in 1908/9 but this book is published to coincide with the beginnings of scouting worldwide in August 2007.

Today's scouts have found out about their long history and are sharing it with others. At the end of the group's first century we are looking back to preserve that heritage as a legacy for scouts of the future.

The founder of scouting in Connah's Quay, E. Ll. Marriott was scoutmaster for thirty-two years until his death aged eighty-seven. When this happened, such was his influence that an emergency meeting was called to see how the scout group would carry on without him. Despite all this, he lay in an unmarked grave for sixty-four years. This was probably because he had no children and died during the war but one of the positive and unexpected outcomes of this project has been the decision to provide a fitting headstone for him. This was done on 4 March 2006.

We have ferreted out facts and been given lots of wonderful photographs for a book. Young scouts and explorers have met and talked with former scouts and recorded interviews as part of an oral history archive and best of all, they have opened up a window into the past; the area around the scout hut has acquired another dimension as they have 'mapped' out the early days of scouting with a heritage trail. Best of all, in two gigantic leaps we have reached back to 1908/9 when the group started. Some of the people interviewed actually made their promises to the first Scoutmaster, Captain Marriott.

Connah's Quay at the Turn of the Century

Connah's Quay was a much smaller place at the beginning of the twentieth century than it is today. The nineteenth-century population of a few hundred had swelled to two thousand, and it was considered to be a boom town.

Known from the time of the Domesday Book by the names of its townships: Wepre, Golftyn, Kelsterton, Leadbrook Major and Leadbrook Minor, it only acquired its present name after the River Dee was canalised and deepened. This tidal section of the river was fixed in its present form by the construction of the new cut from Chester to Golftyn, between 1735 and 1736.

It was first called New Quay, but to avoid mix-ups with other ports of the same name was re-christened Connah's Quay. The area flourished under the Irish Coal Company in the early nineteenth century, and the transport of bricks from Buckley. It further expanded with the arrival of the railway.

Apart from being a route to the port, Connah's Quay grew as a town from the middle of the nineteenth century when ship-building and chemical manufacturing industries set up along the

New industry on the banks of the River Dee.

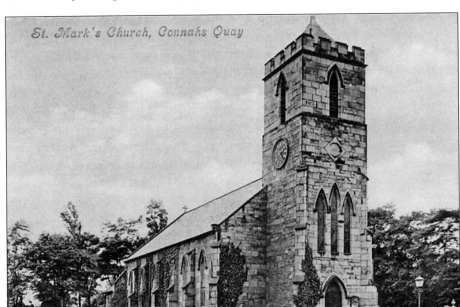

St. Marks Church.

river bank. The traditional occupations of fisherman and agricultural labourer were gradually overtaken by factory-based jobs. New industry brought new people with it.

Their spiritual needs were taken care of by the Golftyn Presbyterian Chapel and St. Mark's Parish Church. Living conditions improved when gas and water were laid on in the 1870s, considerably earlier than Flint and Holywell. The arrival of John Summers' Ironworks heralded a new era of industrial development in the area and this led to further population growth.

The Urban District Council was formed in 1896 and the councillors addressed themselves to the problems created by urbanisation. School accommodation, for instance, was urgently needed in the rapidly developing area. Newspapers reported that due to industrial expansion on the banks of the Dee, Queensferry, Shotton and Connah's Quay had become a dumping ground for families.

Mr James Reney, a member of one of the shipping families of Connah's Quay, maintained that there was no open space for children to play without trespassing, and that the main street was congested by traffic. He proposed a recreation place for youngsters. At the Wesleyan Chapel in Golftyn, the congregation had grown to such dimensions that additional accommodation had to be found in the spacious schoolroom.

The social life of the town was affected by these larger numbers of people when it came to entertainment and recreation. Numerous clubs and societies flourished in the town, and they all had their holidays when their members would take to the streets with dancing and processions. On the sporting side, cycling, walking and football were very popular. Connah's Quay had a football club which hosted an annual sports day. One-mile bicycle races and walking contests were held, and the annual race from Shotton to Rhyl was promoted by workmen and officials from Summers' Iron Works. The sixteen-mile route was from Connah's Quay through Flint, Northop, Ewloe and finished in Hawarden.

Fundraising for good causes was always important. In the days before the National Health Service, medical care was funded by the community and a Nursing Association existed in Connah's Quay. The main fundraiser was the annual Cycle Carnival which started in 1902. These were elaborate parades held on a Wednesday evening, with themed tableaux. They were very successful and newspapers reported that the excitement was so intense 'that people packed the main street like herrings'. Connah's Quay was a town of sea captains, and one hundred years ago the river and its banks were used frequently for social reasons; it was the centre of activity. There were regular pleasure cruises sailing from Connah's Quay to Chester.

One of the captains, Mr Coppack, wrote to the Carnegie Foundation for help with the building of a free library similar to the one at Buckley. The establishment of a library in Connah's Quay was deemed to be a necessity due to its rapid growth, which was phenomenal. Local inhabitants were keen to promote the cultural life of the town as well as trying to find a solution to social problems such as housing. During this period a large part of the Freme estate at Wepre, which had been used until then for agricultural purposes, was rapidly converted into eligible building sites.

Processions at Connah's Quay. In the picture on the left it looks as if the whole town has turned out to see the parade headed by a military band, the firemen and civic dignitaries.

The New Harbour Master Arrives

Connah's Quay had always been a town of great maritime importance and its status increased as the river ceased to be navigable nearer to Chester. It became the premier port of the river Dee with its own harbour master, a position which became vacant at the beginning of the twentieth century.

It was filled by Lieutenant-Commander E. Ll. Marriott, a native of Halifax, who arrived in Connah's Quay with his wife in 1903. He took up the position as Harbour Master, Customs and Excise Officer and Registrar for the Port of Chester. He was aged forty- eight and had previously served in Fleetwood, Hull, Leeds and Liverpool. This was to be his last posting. At first the Marriotts lived at Park Hill, but later moved to 22 Church Street in Connah's Quay.

The docks and harbour area at Connah's Quay was a bustling place with schooners being used to export huge amounts of coal and bricks, and with ship-building and other industries being carried on at the water's edge.

Lieutenant-Commander Edward Llewellyn Marriott, RNR.

Some of the ships that Marriott dealt with had been built in Connah's Quay: the *Maude, Perseverance, Lavinia, Renown, Catherine Latham, Lizzie May, Earl of Beaconsfield, Malvina, Doon* and *Fleurita*. A few of these are remembered today as street names.

As well as a place of business, the riverside was also a social centre. Occasionally local business provided entertainment, such as the day the auctioneer T. S. Adams organised the sale of three sailing ships on the shore; this caused great interest, and large crowds gathered. The beach was a playground for local children and sometimes promenade concerts were staged there.

In 1908 a Chair Eisteddfodd was held at Connah's Quay and Walter Reney, chairman of the Urban

Above: The beach at Connah's Quay.

Right: The docks at Connah's Quay.

District Council, said that he was, 'Greatly pleased to welcome people to our town on the banks of the Dee or, as it has been called, the City of the Future!'

However, Connah's Quay did not have all the qualities of a metropolis and some people complained that it was a dead town by 10 o'clock at night. The town retired so early that when the football club held a supper at the Halfway House an extension was granted only until 10.30pm. In contrast, Connah's Quay UDC protested about the post office changing its closing time from 9pm to 8pm. They feared that the postal service was not as good as other areas.

The year 1908 also saw the formation of both the Wepre Mutual Improvement Society and the Temperance Society. There was an air of general philanthropy in Connah's Quay as people tried to improve their lives and that of their town. E. Ll. Marriott was amongst those who made a difference. He supported the Nursing Association to which his wife belonged as a volunteer nurse, and he also taught in the Evening Technical Classes which were held in St. Mark's and Custom House Lane Schools. It was recognised that adults needed training to learn the skills for new industry. Marriott acted as both teacher and secretary for the St. Mark's evening classes. He taught the building construction class at the rate of 7s. 6d. an hour. Other classes included machine construction, applied mechanics, ambulance and navigation. It was reported in the Education Minutes that instruction in navigation had been offered for any boys from Connah's Quay who intended to choose the calling of a sailor. Three lads had availed themselves of the offer. Afterwards one became a chemist, one a sailor and the other steered his way through Mr John Summers' Iron Works! The committee decided that another fiasco such as this must be

Connah's Quay fishermen.

avoided by improving the association between employers and the county schools.

The Education Minutes mentioned a complaint by E. Ll. Marriott about people using the classroom on other evenings; apparently the local band used it for practising and their smoking and spitting caused damage to the gas mantles!

The area suffered from a depression in trade for some time as did the rest of the country, and some Connah's Quay mothers blamed this when they were summonsed for failing to send their children to school. It was a time of poverty and hardship, but also of much new industry and civic improvements. The Golftyn Provinder Mill was taken over by a new owner who fitted it out with powerful new machinery capable of grinding and crushing large quantities of oats and corn. Summers' Iron and Steel Works was reported to be in full swing, and a new manure works was opened in Connah's Quay.

Less than a year later, however there was a strike at John Summers. In May, the men marched to Mold complaining that they were being treated as slaves because their employers wanted them to work an extra quarter of an hour. In August there was more unrest when the steelworkers demonstrated. Led by a brass band, they walked in procession from the Hare & Hounds to Lloyd's field, via Golftyn Lane and Shotton Lane.

The river continued to play a big part in the life of the area but, despite its canalisation, there were still problems with silting; it was impossible for vessels of even moderate tonnage to come alongside as far as Chester and in 1910 there was talk of the deepening of the Dee. However, fishing continued to be one of the main occupations and in 1908 the story of the forty-one pound salmon made headlines. It was caught by two fishermen in Connah's Quay, William Taylor and John Hewitt, and purchased by the proprieter of the Westminster Hotel in Chester.

There were other areas of the town where recreation could be found apart from the river; Connah's Quay had its own shooting range, and in 1909 a new bowling green was opened at the Conservative Club. E. Ll. Marriott was a founder-member of this and the first match was played against Chester. Connah's Quay lost 70-95, but the newspaper reported cheerfully that it could have been much worse, since only two members of the team, Messrs E. Ll. Marriott and

C. Dawson, had ever handled woods before!

For a few years there had been no Annual Cycle Carnival, but in 1909 Connah's Quay Town Council revived the tradition. A committee was formed with Mr E. D. Blane as president and Mr E. Ll. Marriott as vice-president. Marriott also became involved in local issues such as the supply of domestic water and the state of roads and footpaths in Connah's Quay which were described as deplorable. It is no coincidence that street paving started in Golftyn, near his home at 22 Church Street.

Civic amenities, recreation and education seemed to be some areas where he made a difference in Connah's Quay. A versatile man of many talents, he also wrote regularly for the *Chester Chronicle* and gave lectures on photography.

However, it was in 1907, when Baden-Powell started the Boy Scout movement, that Marriott found a cause that appealed wholeheartedly to him and to which he remained devoted for the rest of his days.

Lord Baden-Powell.

Baden-Powell and Marriott were contemporaries; they were born and died within two years of each other. They also both had military backgrounds. In the early days of Scouting, scoutmasters were usually clergymen or teachers; people in authority. The movement was also supported by the gentry which was of great importance for the provision of campsites. Although Marriott had a naval background and Baden-Powell an army one, stories of Mafeking and the skills of those first 'scouts' made a deep impression on Marriott and it was not long before Connah's Quay folk spotted their harbour master tracking with his first Boy Scouts along the banks of the River Dee. Perhaps because of his naval connection, Marriott was always called 'Captain' by the lads.

'Captain' Marriott's Boy Scout Troop

It is not clear exactly when Marriott started his Boy Scout Troop in Connah's Quay. A page of a logbook has survived with the words, 'April 18th 1908. The formation of my first Troop, 1st Connah's Quay' clearly inscribed and although not signed, it is in Marriott's hand. It is the same writing as the signature in the port of Chester Registrar's logs which were kept by Marriott between 1903 and 1915.

Baden-Powell had started his scouting experiment, with just twenty boys, at Brownsea Island in Dorset in 1907, and the idea took off so rapidly that within two years 11,000 Boy Scouts attended a rally at the Crystal Palace. Everyone knew about scouting and E. Ll. Marriott seems to have become interested not long after it started and had been attempting to form a troop in Connah's Quay. This may have taken some time to achieve, because one of the main drawbacks

Left: Page of Captain Marriott's Scout Troop log book.

Right: Page of a Port of Chester Shipping Register.

20

was not having a place to meet. Also, Marriott was involved in getting scouting up and running in a wider area. One of his scouts, Gilbert Butler, remembers his being involved with troops in Birkenhead and Liverpool. Birkenhead is thought to be where Baden-Powell started scouting officially after the Brownsea Island experimental camp.

Marriott's address book has details of other scoutmasters, and even more revealing is his 'birthday book' in which his friends were invited to sign their own names on their birthdays. The entry for 22 February is in the unmistakable bold hand of Baden-Powell, proving that they were more than mere acquaintances. However, the only firm evidence of when scouting started in Connah's Quay is a newspaper report from the *Flintshire Observer*, 11 February 1910:

A troop of boy Scouts is now being formed under the superintendence of Lt. Comm. E. Ll. Marriott. When completed this will form a local patrol under the auspices of the South Flintshire Boy Scouts Association, the HQ of which is at Hawarden. According to the Lieutenant [sic], there is an abundance of excellent material to hand and therefore he is sure of the right stuff. The lads are trained to act independently and on their own initiative and books bearing on the training intended are available which would be of great interest to the average boy. It is thought that the move will be a great success and that the lads will benefit physically and mentally thereby.

That was the troop 'going public' and the reason was that Marriott was involved in organising a huge event that would project Connah's Quay Boy Scouts onto a national stage. Plans were afoot to invite Baden-Powell to Flintshire.

Exactly one month after the announcement of the Connah's Quay Troop being formed, the *Flintshire News* reported a meeting at Hawarden County School of the Hawarden/South Flintshire Boy Scouts Association which included E. Ll. Marriott, Messrs Lyon, Marston and Gregory, and the vicar of Mold, The purpose was to get the association into thorough working order, and to induce the 'well-known Scouting Master, General Baden-Powell to attend a battalion parade comprising the troops of Bagillt, Holywell, Flint, Connah's Quay, Hawarden,

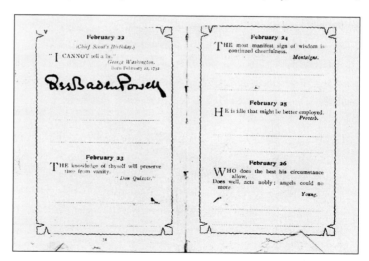

Captain Marriott's Birthday Book.

Start of Scouting tablet found in Birkenhead.

Mold and Caergwrle'. These efforts were successful and in April the newspaper reported that:

Lt. General Baden-Powell will make a tour of north Wales at the beginning of May for the purpose of encouraging and more fully organising the boy scouts movement. As at present arranged he will devote May 2nd to Flintshire and Denbighshire and on the following day, different centres in Caernavonshire. On May 4th he will go to Anglesey speaking in Holyhead on the evening of the same day. As is the case almost everywhere, scouting, although still in its infancy, has taken a firm hold in north Wales and such an excellent life-giving movement should be encouraged. It will be with the object of giving the movement an impetus that Baden-Powell's visit has been arranged. The organisation of the movement in Anglesey is making rapid headway. Lord Lt. Sir R. Williams-Bulkley is evincing considerable interest in the movement as is the Marquis of Anglesey, the Rt. Hon Lord Boston, Comm. Holland, and many other influential gentlemen.

This event caused considerable excitement and great efforts were made to present a smart appearance. The *Flintshire News* noted that:

The Connah's Quay Boy Scouts are making good headway and it is pleasing to note that they are now in possession of a uniform, each boy having secured his own. Scoutmaster Marriott is deserving of every encouragement in the interest he is showing towards the lads.

'Captain' Marriott worked at creating a Boy Scout Troop in Connah's Quay and was instrumental in bringing Baden-Powell to Flintshire to inspect the Welsh troops for the first time in 1910. On Monday 6 May, the great day dawned and Baden-Powell made his visit. As a preliminary, Connah's Quay Boy Scouts had been on parade in Holywell the Saturday before and they were able to figure prominently in the inspection at Hawarden.

The hero of Mafeking inspected the boy scouts of Flintshire at Hawarden on Monday. 270 boys were on parade from all parts of Flintshire also Chester, Wrexham and Gresford. Mr Lyn, Head of Hawarden County School was in command and many of the patrols were in the charge of district clergy or members of the teaching profession. The review took place on the spacious playing field of the county school into which crowded a large number of the public. The General (Baden-Powell) accompanied by his private secretary, Mr Walker, and accompanied by Cl. Howard, CB and Major J. H. Wynne Eyton, was warmly welcomed by the young soldiers.

1ST CONNAH'S QUAY B.P. BOY SCOUTS

HUT, BRICKFIELDS,
opposite Fountain,
off High Street,
CONNAH'S QUAY

Lieut. Commdr.
E. L. MARRIOTT, R.N.R.
Scoutmaster,
22 CHURCH STREET,
CONNAH'S QUAY,
Flintshire.

H. BUTLER,
A.S.M. and Cubmaster,
3 Pen-y-llan Street.

The Chief Scout inspecting the 1st Connah's Quay Troop at the Hawarden Rally, May 2nd, 1910.
By courtesy of "The Scouter."

1st Connah's Quay Scout Group letterhead with an indistinct picture of the Hawarden Rally on it.

Members of the Flintshire Constabulary were on duty in their dress uniform and Buckley CLB band played. Afterwards, in the school, Baden-Powell delivered a lengthy address to a large number of people including old soldiers with medals pinned to their breasts. Chair, Major Wynne Eyton introduced Baden-Powell and mentioned that he was the inventor of the Boy Scout movement. The way in which the scheme had progressed in its short life was simply marvellous.

A picture of this event in Hawarden was used as part of the letterhead of 1st Connah's Quay Scout Group for many years. Marriott's influence was important enough to make Connah's Quay a major player in the South Flintshire District. The County Treasurer banked the Scout funds in Connah's Quay.

However, the troop did not have a base and when they met it was usually out of doors. At last, in November 1910, 'Captain' Marriott obtained use of a reading room for the boys where he encouraged them to study the scouting manuals he had acquired; education was very important to him.

Marriott was Assistant Commissioner and Hon. Secretary of the South Flintshire Boy Scouts Association, and the *Flintshire Observer* reported a meeting where he spoke of the difficulty of getting leaders to start the troops in the county. It was decided to hold a series of displays sometime in the middle of February in Connah's Quay, and to raise a troop to travel round and give those displays. The one in Connah's Quay took place in March 1911 where, it was reported:

Captain Marriott's exhibition in aid of scouting 1911.

BOY SCOUTS.—In aid of the funds of the 1st Connah's Quay troop of Boy Scouts, a camp fire and exhibition of curiosities from many lands is being held this week in the room at 332a High-street. The arrangements had been carried out by Lieut. E. Ll. Marriott, who is the enthusiastic scoutmaster, Alderman E. Blane opened the exhibition on Monday. The scoutmaster gave an explanation of the boy scout movement, describing its aims, objects and organisation. Mr Blane spoke about the organisation and the success of the troop and gave a handsome subscription towards the funds. He highly complimented Lieutenant and Mrs Marriott on the collection of objects which had been obtained in the district, expressing suprise that so many interesting things had been hidden in their midst and no one knew anything about them. He formally declared the exhibition opened. Rev Daniel Marriott also spoke of the good work done by the scout master, Lieut. Marriott and said some very encouraging words to the boys. Exhibits were lent by Mr Blane, Rev Dr Hook, Captain Alletson, Mr James Baird, Mr Frank Baird, and Mrs Jesse Baird Jones. Captains Conway, Coppack, Carter and Bennett sent models of steamers and sailing vessels. Mr Tyrrell, Mrs Hampson, and Captain W. E. Griffiths, R.N.R., sent various objects from the West coast of Africa which were particularly interesting. Mrs E. Ll. Marriott's collection of arms and armour and old china were much admired. The exhibition was well patronised during the week and remains open until Saturday. It is well worth a visit.

Tho congratulations of the Connah's Quay Boy Scout Patrol were wired to H.R.H. the Prince of Wales upon the occasion of his birthday on Sunday last. We give below the text of the telegram and the reply:—H.R.H. Prince of Wales, Buckingham Palace. The Connah's Quay North Wales Boy Scouts beg most respectfully to offer to you, our chief scout, their heartfelt congratulations on your birthday, E. Ll. Marriott, Scoutmaster. Reply: Windsor Castle, June 23, 1912. Scoutmaster, Boy Scouts, Connah's Quay, North Wales.—I am desired by the Prince of Wales to thank the Connah's Quay Boy Scouts for their kind congratulations. "Equerry."

CONNAH'S QUAY.

The Boy Scouts send a birthday telegram to the Prince of Wales and receive a reply.

A campfire and exhibition of curiosities and historical relics from many lands was held at 302a High Street in aid of Boy Scout funds. Alderman Blane opened the exhibition and spoke of the organisation and success of the troop. He also gave a handsome subscription. The arrangements were made by E. Ll. Marriott described as the enthusiastic scoutmaster and he gave an explanation of the Boy Scout movement and its aims. The Rev. D. Marriott from Goftyn Chapel (no relation) was also present and he spoke encouragingly to the boys. Items for the exhibition were loaned by Mr Blane, the Rev. D. Hook, Mr J. Baird, Mr. Frank Baird,, Mrs Jessie Baird Jones. Captains Conway, Coppack, Carter and Bennett sent models of ships, steamers and sailing vessels. Mrs Tyrrell, Mrs Hampson and Captain W. E. Griffiths, RNR, sent objects from the west coast of Africa. Mrs Marriott's collection of arms and armour and old china was much admired. The exhibition was open for a week and according to the newspapers, was well worth a visit.

The success of this exhibition was probably measured in terms of prestige as well as finance. The Scout movement was being brought to the attention of the wider public in an attempt to attract publicity and support.

The *Flintshire News* ran a weekly column called 'Scouts' Corner' written by someone calling himself 'Haversack'. It was full of scouting tips and news; 'Captain' Marriott featured regularly in it.

1911 was an eventful year for the Connah's Quay Boy Scouts. In June, a menagerie came to town and people were treated to the spectacle of wild animals parading through the streets; there were hyenas, wolves, bears, tigers, camels, twenty lions and four elephants. One event was a test of strength … thirty men against one elephant.

In July 1911 'Captain' Marriott took sixteen Scouts to the King's Rally at Windsor. This was a month after the coronation of King George V and was a huge gathering of Scouts. Transport arrangements were made with military precision for the 29,000 boys who descended upon London for the day from Britain and abroad. On this occasion the Prince of Wales was made Chief Scout for Wales and the following year 'Captain' Marriott sent him a telegram wishing him a happy birthday from Connah's Quay Boy Scouts.

In September, 'Captain' Marriott took the boy scouts for a trip up river to Chester accompanied by Scoutmaster Day. This was aboard the motorboat *Surprise*, kindly provided by the Messrs Garrett, Coppack & Williams.

In November, a new Boy Scout room was opened at 25 Dock Road, Connah's Quay. The ceremony was performed by Dr Hook, County Secretary of the Boy Scout Association, and he spoke of:

One of the bell-tents in Wepre Woods. The Troop obtained permission from local land-owners, such as the Fremes of Wepre, to camp on their land.

The importance in having rooms for the boys in which to teach skills and stressed how it would help to prevent boys running to waste for want of guidance.

The movement was seen as a remedy for many social problems.

The Scouts gradually became part of the life of the town and people became used to their activities and depended on their participation in civic events. In 1912 they were present at Flint Castle when it was made the Headquarters of the 5th Battalion, Royal Welsh Fusiliers. Empire Day in 1913 was celebrated by Connah's Quay Girl Guides and Boy Scouts at Park Hill near the Marriott home.

After saluting the flag and the march past, Scoutmaster E. Ll. Marriott, on behalf of the boy scouts, presented a silver medal to Edwin Grimes, aged eleven, for pluckily saving a boy from drowning in Connah's Quay docks. This was followed by an exhibition of bridge building and lifesaving drills. Afterwards tea was provided by Mrs Marriott and the remainder of the evening spent in games and tug of war, with the House Patrol v the Woodpigeons.

They joined in every public ceremony from carnivals to church parade and newspaper reports about the boy scouts always contained the telling phrase … 'Scoutmaster Marriott in charge'. According to a census taken in September 1913, there were fourteen Scouts in Connah's Quay.

The Scouts marched everywhere and enjoyed the hospitality of several local landowners who gave them permission to camp on their land.

In 1914 the Scouts camped at least twice; their summer camp was held under canvas at Highfield Hall, and before they left they presented their host, Miss Corelli, with a 'Thanks' badge for her interest and support for the troop. Wepre woods were not open to the public, but

John Rowden Freme, last owner of Wepre Hall, gave his permission for the boys to camp there. In 1914, they found a sixteenth-century duelling sword in the woods which they cleaned, mounted and presented to the Fremes. How exciting that must have been for them, knowing that they were probably penetrating areas where no one else had set foot for centuries, and of course 'Captain' Marriott's appreciation of history would have made their find memorable. It was such a good story that it actually appeared in Mr Freme's obituary notice five years later.

The First World War

When the First World War broke out, Lt.-Cmr. Marriott was very busy dealing with members of the RNR who reported themselves for duty from various vessels in the port. Men were paid off by their skippers and reported to Connah's Quay Customs Office which was in the bank buildings on Church Hill. There, they were received by Marriott, who examined their Naval Reserve Certificates. He then, as registrar, completed the necessary formalities, handed over their retaining fees and witnessed them depart by the first available trains to take up duties in the Royal Navy. He was also the shipping intelligence officer for the coast between Chester and Llandudno.

Mrs Marriott was also involved in war work as a voluntary nurse at Leeswood Hall which housed a military hospital during the First world War. On one occasion she took injured soldiers from there on a trip by charabanc to the Hippodrome Picture House in Connah's Quay, then afterwards gave them tea at St. Mark's Hall where the silver band played for them before their return to Leeswood.

Despite these heavy commitments, Marriott seems to have been able to keep the Boy Scouts running and in the best spirit of Scouting the lads made themselves useful. Indeed, at least one of them saw military action and sadly, the first military funeral was of former Scout, Ben Dutton, in January 1915. Hundreds of people turned out for his funeral procession. The *Chester Chronicle* reported the event:

Lance Corporal Ben Dutton from Ash Grove, Shotton had volunteered for active service in the Royal Welsh Fusiliers.

Message of thanks from Lord Baden-Powell.

To 1st Connah's Quay B.P .Boy Scouts.

I want to thank you for helping to give friendly shelter and assistance to our distressed refugee brothers

Baden Powell

He had been in the trenches for two days when he had suffered serious injuries. He was brought back to the Manchester Military Hospital where he died on 29 December 1914. At his funeral in early January there was an immense crowd of 1,000 people in the main street. The procession marched to the United Methodist Church in Connah's Quay. The firing party was composed of men serving as guards from the concentration camp at Queensferry. They carried their arms in customary reverse order. There was the usual volley of shots at Bryn Road cemetery. Connah's Quay Boy Scouts, of whom Ben had been a member under the charge of Captain Marriott, formed a ring and kept the space at the graveside.

Throughout the First World War, the Boy Scouts continued to meet and do invaluable work towards the war effort. They earned a special message from Baden-Powell. In 1917 they had a waste-paper collection and raised £6 8s. 2d. This sum was spent on a personal weighing machine for Leeswood Military Hospital. Among the collection were some old books which Marriott had the presence of mind to send to the National Library at Aberystwyth. He recognised that the books were very rare seventeenth-century Welsh theological works. At the time a newspaper reported that, 'if it had not been for the foresight of Mr Marriott, they would now be pulp'.

When the war ended, the Scouts, along with the rest of the community, joined in with the Peace Day celebrations:

School children assembled outside the drill hall with the Connah's Quay silver band in attendance. There were a number of themes displayed upon lorries and horse-drawn traps. In one tableau boys were dressed as soldiers, with Turkish and German prisoners. Girls were dressed as Britannia and her attendants. One lorry carried an imitation submarine. Many of the scholars wore fancy dress and behind the band marched Mr Marriot's scouts followed by pony traps carrying the civic dignitaries.

At a Town Council meeting in November 1919, Lt.-Cmr. Marriott brought up the subject of the Poppy Day collection. He had forwarded the proceeds of a collection, which amounted to £7 12s. 0d., to the Earl Haig Memorial Fund. He urged the Council to establish a War Memorial on Deeside to which people could make a pilgrimage and lay their wreaths as in other Flintshire towns. This took ten years to come to fruition.

War Memorial for Connah's Quay and Shotton.

Celebrating the Twenties

Marriott found a new outlet for his energies as he grew nearer to retirement age. He had been due to retire in 1915, but had patriotically decided to stay on, owing to the great shortage of officers in the Service. He was a man with many titles when he officially retired in 1919. He was listed as being the Principal Customs Officer for the port of Chester, Registrar of Shipping and Receiver of Wrecks, Superintendent of Mercantile Marines and Paymaster of the RNR. He was also the Honorary Secretary of Connah's Quay and Flint National Lifeboat Institute. After retirement he stayed on in Connah's Quay where he had finally put down roots. He had made many friends there and indeed, had become a stalwart of the community. Apart from Scouts he was secretary and treasurer of several other organisations including his wife's Nursing Association.

At an age when most people wound down, Marriott remained active in Scouting and was in contact with many Scout groups in Wales, Cheshire and Lancashire. It is possible that when his work with the Royal Navy ended he re-directed all of his skills and experience into the Scout group. In 1919, local registration of groups transferred to Gilwell, the Scout headquarters.

In the 1920s, there was a great deal of Scout activity. The First World War had prevented the movement from celebrating its tenth anniversary but it was marked belatedly in 1920 with the first World Jamboree at Olympia in London. Only four years later, the second World Jamboree was held in Copenhagen. The same summer there was a British Empire Exhibition at Wembley and a Scout Rally was held at the same time. This turned into a jamboree as well, with 10,000 scouts camping in Wembley Paddocks for ten days — the largest Boy Scout camp ever seen. As Assistant Commissioner, Marriott organised the contingent travelling from Flintshire.

'Captain' Marriott at the time he retired from the posts of Harbour Master and Customs and Excise Officer.

THE BOY SCOUTS ASSOCIATION.

Form F.

ANNUAL GROUP RE-REGISTRATION.   AS ON 30th. SEPTEMBER 1928.

This form is only to be used for renewal until 30th September 1929 of registration already effected.

COUNTY *Flintshire*   LOCAL ASSOCIATION *South Flint (Deeside)*

NOTE :-   The officer in charge of Group is requested to complete this form and return it not later than October 3rd to the Hon. Secretary of the Local Association (who will forward it, through the County Secretary, to Imperial Headquarters).   The Group will then be re-registered until the 30th September 1929 and notification of this will be sent to the officer through the Secretary of the Local Association. Only Groups registered at Imperial Headquarters will be recognised.

Group Title as registered at I.H.Q. :- *1st Connah's Quay*   I.H.Q. No *6405*

GROUP OFFICERS.

Warranted or on Probation: the latter must be starred ★.

Rank.	Name.	Address.
Group S. M.		
Scoutmaster	*E. L. Marriott*	*22 Church Street Connah's Quay Flintshire*
Cubmaster		
Rover Leader		
A. S. M.		
A. C. M.		
A. R. L.		

Enter in this space which, if any, of the following applies to the Group:- Works Group, Deaf, Blind or otherwise disabled Scouts, School, Industrial School, Home, Orphanage, &c.

Signed *E. L. Marriott*   Group S.M. (or officer in charge).

Date *1 October 1928*

Re-Registered at Imperial Headquarters on ....

New Number .... by ....

Those holding more than One warrant or Officers who are also Rovers should only be counted once.

NUMBERS.

Warranted :-			
Group S.M.		Scouts	6
S.M. & A.S.M's.	1	Sea Scouts	
C.M. & A.C.M's.		Wolf Cubs	
R.L. & A.R.L's.		Rover Scouts	
★ Total On Probation.		Rover Sea Scouts	
No of Scouters	1	No. of Scouters	1
		Group Total.	7

Group re-registered in 1928.

There were 950 scouts and leaders. Large scale national events were always preceded by local ones and this was no exception. There was a rally at Queensferry which Marriott did not attend; he was probably too busy making plans for Wembley.

The *Flintshire Chronicle* reported on a fundraising event in 1927.

To augment funds of St. David's Church in Mold Road there was a revue at the Institute by the Boy Scout Players called 'The Reveille'. All the actors were members of 1st Connah's Quay Boy Scouts. Much mirth was created by this production of a clever and refined show of ventriloquists, impressionists, singers and comedians.

In 1928, the Flintshire Boy Scouts Association was formed, and in recognition of his hard work and dedication over almost twenty years, Lt.-Cmr. Marriott was awarded the Medal of Merit for his outstanding work with the Boy Scout movement. This was presented at Hawarden Castle by Sir Robert Baden-Powell.

Also in 1928, the system for recording the numbers of groups was changed at national headquarters at Gilwell. Scouts and Wolf Cubs, who had been recorded separately, were now joined and all groups obliged to re-register. Connah's Quay Scout Group records at this time show that numbers were very low. Only seven scouts and one scoutmaster were recorded. Perhaps this was an indication of the economic depression of the inter-war years. Trade figures for Connah's Quay dropped to a third in 1928 from what they had been before the war and the Chamber of Shipping declared the port was to be 'run-down'. A deputation of Connah's Quay town councillors joined with Flintshire MPs and the local Board of Trade in a deputation to London to protest about the Railway Bill to close down Connah's Quay as a port. However, three

Poster for the Jamboree at Arrowe Park, Birkenhead.

Arrowe Park, 1929.

Jack Evans, Don Grundy and Iowerth Jones at Arrowe Park

Connah's Quay scouts managed to attend the third World Jamboree at Birkenhead in 1929 when scouting came of age even though the Flintshire Scout Council Annual Report shows that they did not have a permanent meeting place. However it is possible that Marriott went to Arrowe Park in his capacity as Assistant Commissioner, because photographs of that event have survived.

Surviving the Thirties

In 1930, after temporary headquarters in various parts of the town, Connah's Quay Boy Scouts celebrated their move to a new permanent home. It was on part of the Red Hall estate almost opposite the Dock Road and near to the clay pit. It was acquired for the troop by Major H. Hughes, manager of the National Provincial Bank. He was also treasurer of the County Association of Boy Scouts. It has been described as, 'an old, corrugated, green shed lined inside with tongue and groove, warmed by a pot-bellied stove and lit by paraffin lamps that hung from a wagon wheel suspended from the ceiling'. It had once been an ironmonger's shop in Shotton and was transported to its new home, where it served the Scout troop well for more than thirty years. Mr Moreton Green donated furniture for the hut and, over a period of time, it was extended no less than five times.

Another cause for celebration was the Golden Wedding Anniversary of Captain and Mrs Marriott in February 1932. They had been married in Hull in 1882. Captain Marriott continued his work with the wider scouting world and was a member of the Scout Council in 1935, when there were six associations, thirty-one groups and seventy-three officers.

Numbers for Connah's Quay had shown no improvement by the mid-thirties. Even though records show that Wolf Cub packs had been running in other parts of the country since 1914, this had not happened at Connah's Quay. The 1935 census for the group was officers 1, Cubs 0, Scouts 7, Rovers 1. It is highly probable that Captain Marriott's advancing years prevented him from encouraging numbers to grow. Towards the end of the decade it was the practice of the scouts to collect their scoutmaster from his house at 22 Church Street and wheel him down to the Scout Hut on the trek cart for the weekly Tuesday meeting. For a short time, he was assisted

Camp at Ellesmere 'The Grange' 1938. Malcolm Brooke-Freeman, Arthur Jones, Tom Roberts, Auntie Mattie, Bill Hutton and Gilbert Butler.

Wolf Cub Tests.

by another scoutmaster, Mr Stretch, but he carried on alone for most of the time. The census figures for 1936 were improved with, officers 1, Cubs 0, Scouts 16, Rovers 0. This increase may have prompted the desire for a better meeting place because in the summer of 1936 plans were submitted to Connah's Quay UDC for a new room. These were inspected and approved.

Gilbert Butler joined the Scouts in 1934. He had seen lads in school wearing the Scout badge and he was curious about it. Little did he know that his curiosity would lead to a lifetime's involvement with 1st Connah's Quay Scouts for Gilbert and his entire family. By 1938, a Wolf Cub pack opened and his two brothers joined. They met at an earlier time on the same night as the scouts. His father and sister became leaders, his mother was on the parents' committee and also acted as housekeeper to Captain and Mrs Marriott. She used to take her younger son, John with her when she worked. John remembers Captain Marriott as being quite different from the strict man down at the Scout Hut. He had games that John was allowed play with. Later on, Gilbert's wife also served on the parents' committee, and his son went through the group as a cub and scout, and eventually became a leader as well.

When Gilbert made his promise to Captain Marriott, he remembers him as being a jovial, very kindly, sociable man who always wore khaki breeches, a safari-style jacket, and a large Scout hat for the meetings. Raymond Gregory joined in 1937:

Very soon after I joined at the age of ten, I was entered for my Tenderfoot Test with another scout. This consisted of a verbal test of the very basic rules of scouting such as the Scout Law and the motto, 'Be Prepared'. It was undertaken at the home of Captain Marriott in Church Street and it was quite an awe-inspiring business as never before had we met such an exalted person! One of the earliest tests I did was to travel on foot from Connah's Quay to Shotton in a certain time using the method of running 50 and walking 50 paces. This was easy for me as I did it every day going to school.

Gordon Henshaw, who made his promise in 1936, remembers there being very little money around and how his parents had saved up to buy him the Scout shirt and hat. The lads always wore boots, never shoes, and all scouts carried a staff. This was a really important piece of equipment used on hikes and at camp several of them could be put together to make bridges.

Whenever the scouts were at camp they utilised as many of the natural features of the outdoors as they could. Camping near water meant they could build fords, swim and catch their

*Camp at Ddol Farm,
St Asaph.*

dinner. Hilly ground meant they could construct aerial runways, the longer the better. The lads would skim down hanging on for dear life!

Gilbert's father, Harry, who had been a scout in his hometown of Ellesmere, became assistant scoutmaster with Captain Marriott, and Gilbert was Patrol Leader. The patrols were called: Peewits, Owls and Hounds. As well as Tuesday meetings in the Scout Hut, the lads met up every weekend. Gilbert's patrol, the Hounds, went to a place known as 'Bluebell Carpet' up on the Buckley Line or to Wepre woods on Saturday afternoons. Sometimes they made a whole weekend camp at Plas Bellin, then in the ownership of the Charlton family. They would push the trek cart, loaded with all their kit, up Mold Road stopping on the way to buy homemade nettle pop to take along for a treat. The Charltons were very generous to the scouts, giving them access to their land for camping and allowing them to keep their equipment in one of the stables. In return the boys helped with some of the seasonal work such as gathering the hay in from the fields. Invariably they were welcomed by the gamekeeper who would present them with a couple of rabbits which would be put in the pot for their Saturday night supper. Ken Taylor recalls conditions at camp:

The group was never rained off. They stuck it out even in the heaviest downpours and wore plimsolls with no socks, never Wellingtons. Once, however, at Plas Bellin everything was washed away and the lads had to shelter in the stables. They thought they were fortunate to find horse blankets to put round themselves only to find themselves scratching for a week … the blankets were full of fleas!

If the troop was not camping, Captain Marriott expected to see them turn out for church parade on Sunday mornings. They would march from the Scout Hut to either church or chapel.

Everything the boys did was designed to help them to be useful citizens and to acquire skills.

Camp at Ellesmere 1939.
Back Row: Ken Taylor, Bill Hutton, Bob Foulkes, Norman Gamblin, Bill Roberts, 'Skip' Butler, Tommy Roberts, Gilbert Butler, Dennis Mannion.
Centre Row: Rennie Shaw, Arthur Jones, Malcolm Freeman, Captain Marriott, John Fellowes, Jack Coppack.
Front Row: Herbert Clarke, Jeff Hughes, Ray Davidson, John Butler, Joe Butler, Gordon Seager, John Taylor.

The system used revolved around badges such as the Pioneer, Ambulance or Cook badge. This was an integral part of scouting and a few of them gained the much prized Bushman's thong and went on to become a King's Scout.

There was a great deal of work to be done in order to gain any of the badges and the lads had to show initiative. Gordon Henshaw tells how he won his cookery badge:

First of all, you needed some pennies to get the stuff … a 'pennorth of bits of scrag end from the butcher's, some mixed veg from Hannah's the greengrocer. You also needed a pinch of salt from home and an empty 2lb tin which you had to fix a little handle to. Then you'd take all that up the hillies, take some water from the brook, boil it all up and hope for the best. Skip would taste it and you'd get the badge.

In 1939, the *Chester Chronicle* reported that Marriott was still Assistant Commissioner and that the 1st Connah's Quay Scouts were still marching with him despite his eighty-five years. In 1938, 30 scouts and 25 cubs went to camp and the following year it was recorded that there were 50 scouts present at the annual camp in Ellesmere, so whether the numbers had increased

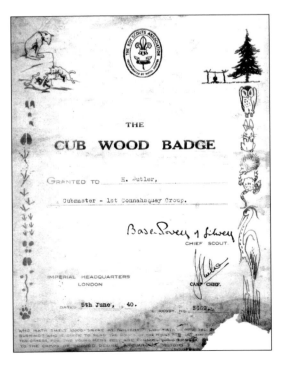

Skip Butler's Wood Badge Certificate.

dramatically or the troop had joined forces with others is unknown. What is certain is that Captain Marriott did have two assistants to help by then — L. A. Williams joined Scoutmaster Butler who was in charge of that camp. Marriott confined his field activities to a visit which is immortalised in the only photograph of him at camp.

The Second World War

In 1939 the Second World War started and men were called up for military service. In December, the Flintshire Boy Scouts Association Handbook revealed that:

The outbreak of war found scouts ready for service. At once they were in great demand in all kinds of Civil Defence work especially at Warden's Posts, Auxiliary Fire Stations and the Evacuation Scheme. Local authorities have been very appreciative of this work.

All scouts joining the services were presented with a small silver wrist badge which they wore throughout the war so that they could recognise other scouts. Wherever they were based they were regarded as a lone scout and not attached to any particular group. Therefore they could join in with any meetings in the area they were stationed; on site, in town or near barracks. Gilbert Butler went to HMS *Royal Arthur* as a signalman. He remembers:

Once a week there was an announcement piped through on a tannoy inviting members of the scout movement to meet in the scout hut on the camp. There were several hundred always present.

Many of the signalmen were former scouts and there is no doubt that the skills learned back in the Scout Hut, such as morse code and semaphore, proved very useful. Gaining proficiency badges was part of the second-class test in scouting. Boys also learned how to knot and splice rope, had ambulance training and did pioneer work. Gilbert Butler soon found out that everything he had done in the Scouts helped during the war. Gordon Henshaw is of the opinion that Scouting served them in good stead during the war; they under-

Boys going to Scouts during the war years.
The Hutton Brothers.

Camp at Ellesmere 1943. Back Row: Joe Butler, Ken Taylor, Gordon Hannah, John Fellows, Bill Hutton, Jim Williams, Mr Dodd. Centre Row: Maldwyn Bates, Ray Gregory, D. Smallman, Dennis Hughes, Jack Coppack, Tommy Lumberg, –?–, Glyn Hewitt, Bob Hutton, Ron Parlane, Ray Jones, Tony Lloyd. Kneeling Row: John Taylor, Gaynor Buckley, Audrey Jones, Skip Butler, Frank Roberts, Glyn Anglesea, Jeff Hannah, Keith Anglesea. Cubs unknown.

stood discipline and were conversant with obeying orders.

It was not only the older boys who were involved as soldiers and sailors. The Chief Scout had written to the Home Secretary offering the services of Scouts and Rover Scouts as messengers. The offer was gratefully received so in Connah's Quay the scouts played an active part. During the evacuation programme they distributed cards to houses telling people how many evacuees they could have. The older boys, 13 and 14 year olds, attended an Air Raid Precautions course at Custom House School, learning about gas masks and tear gas. They were all awarded their ARP badges and undertook serious responsibilities. When they were on duty, they had to wear their Scout uniform in school in case they were called upon. Along with the rest of the country, they prepared for the blitz, and one of the exercises was practising for the real thing. The first Flintshire blackout was a complete success. This was reported in the newspaper:

At 12.30 am everywhere was plunged into darkness. The ARP Auxiliary, Fire Brigade, Ambulances, First Aid Teams, Decontamination Squads and the Boy Scouts carrying out duties as messengers on their bicycles, all ready for their allotted tasks. The mock situations they attended were 1. Casualties at Breeze Hill where there were high explosive bombs. 2. A fire at the Halfway House. 3. A poison gas bomb at the river bank in the vicinity of the Black Works (Joseph Turner's tar works) near the Queensferry Bridge. The four warden posts were Bennett and

*Camp at Ellesmere 1945. Back Row: John Roberts, Jack Coppack, Ray Gregory, Skip Butler,
Glyn Anglesea, Ken Taylor, Manfred Landau, D. Smallman, Gordon Hannah, Ron Parlane.
Centre Row: Jeff Hannah, –?–, Bill Peters,Unknown, Richie Parry, Bob Hutton, –?–, –?–,
J. Butler. Front Row: –?–, Roy Taylor, Ron Bennett, John Taylor, –?–, Pat Hogan, Fred Shaw,
Herbie Martin, –?– Butler.*

Arnold's Garage, the electrical engineer's house at Breeze Hill, and Shotton and Queensferry
police stations.

   The advent of the war did not stop the scouts carrying on with their usual activities although
there were differences. The Wednesday evening meetings continued at the Scout Hut. One boy
remembers the night he walked home after one of these with a couple of friends and a piece of
shrapnel crashing onto a hedge took a piece out of his Scout hat!

   The boys made their own fun in the old tin hut and kept the traditions going. There were
pantomimes at Christmas and concerts with scripts that they made up themselves usually on
topical war themes. The war effort was important and the boys collected waste paper and glass
which was stored in skips outside the Scout Hut and they continued to go to camp although
there was food rationing just as there was at home. One of these camps was at Chirk where the
boys camped in the castle grounds, another was at the official camp site for Wales in Denbigh
where there was an outdoor swimming pool which was fed by a mountain stream. The boys
used it only once as it was so bitterly cold. Camping at Ellesmere was still popular because it
was the home of Harry Butler; his parents ran a smallholding there, and he combined visiting
his family with summer Scout camp during his annual holiday. John Butler remembers his

mother going to camp with them and of there being a plentiful supply of vegetables and eggs.

The 1940 Flintshire Scout Association records show that the treasurer of 1st Connah's Quay Scouts was J. Hughes of the National Westminster Bank and that Lt.-Cmr. Marriott was a member of the executive committee. This is the first indication that there was now a 2nd Connah's Quay troop. Among the list of examiners the names of E. Ll. Marriott, GSM, appeared for Connah's Quay, and the Reverend W. J. Bennett for 2nd Connah's Quay which met at the St. David's Parish Room. This meant that at the grand age of eighty-five, Captain Marriott had finally given up the role of Scoutmaster, only to take up the greater position of Group Scout Master.

In the same year the Deeside Red Cross purchased a mobile First Aid van. This was officially christened, *Florence Nightingale* by the President of the Flintshire Red Cross, Lady Mainwaring, at a rally at the Garthorpe field. The Connah's Quay Scout troops were in attendance and the newspapers reported that the oldest troop in the county was led by Captain Marriott who, despite his years was still as keen as ever.

In late 1941, Mrs Marriott died aged eighty-one years and Captain Marriott was not seen again in public; his many committees had then to function without him. Reports were not produced, and apologies were made for his indisposition. The Scout group had to continue without him as he fell into a decline after the death of his wife. He died just four months later, and on 9 April 1942, the Scouts carried his coffin to its resting place in Connah's Quay Cemetery as they had done for his wife such a short time before. For the Scout group there was a great void left by the death of Captain Marriott. In May, they held an emergency meeting to fill the vacancy. There were tributes to his life and work from Messrs Coppack, Hannah and Parlane. The Marriott house

The sale of the Marriott's household effects.

By Instructions of the Reps. of the late Lt.-Comdr. E. L. Marriott.

DEAN MOUNT VILLA. 22 CHURCH ST, CONNAH'S QUAY

IMPORTANT SALE of the Whole of the HOUSEHOLD

FURNISHINGS
CURIOS
& GENERAL EFFECTS
briefly comprising

Grand toned Piano in walnut case by 'Gors and Kallman,' 3-piece Settee Suite in grey moquette, 4ft. Oak Bookcase and Books, Lounge and Fireside Chairs, Old Pewter, Brass Items, Lustre and other China, Pictures, Glass, Antique Mahogany Drop Leaf Table, Sheraton China Cabinet, Small Antique Chest of Drawers, Battery Wireless Set, Oak Hall Stand, Antique Rifles, Revolvers, Swords, Spears, Bugles, Spurs, etc., Old Mahogany Card Table, Mahogany Sideboard fitted with cupboards and drawers, Oak Dinner Wagon, Brussels and other Carpets and Rugs, Gilt Mirrors, 3ft. 6ins. Mahogany Bureau, Mahogany Bookcase with glazed doors, Hand Sewing Machine, 5ft. INLAID OLD OAK WELSH DRESSER, fitted with 2 small side glazed cupboards together with 3 drawers and cupboards below with the Pattern Dishes and Plates, Antique Spindle-back Arm-chair, 7-piece Carved Walnut Suite in tapestry, 4 Mahogany Chests of Drawers, Oak and Japanned Bedsteads, Spring and Hair Mattresses, Bolsters and Pillows, Curtains, Mahog. Half Bedroom Suites, Ottoman Couch, Mahy. Round Table, Valuable Stand and Hand Cameras, Towel Airers and Toilet Ware, Mahogany Dining Table, Toilet Mirrors, Camp Beds, Kitchen Furnishings, Dinner and Tea Crockery, Cooking Utensils, Wringer, Galvanised Baths and Buckets, Step Ladders, 2 Bags and Golf Clubs, Various Games, Mandoline in case, Work Bench with iron vice, Joiners' and Garden Tools, Model Yacht and numerous other items.

On FRIDAY, MAY 8th, 1942.
SALE at 12 o'clock Sharp.

and furnishings were sold off, and the sale catalogue revealed the richness of their lives and interests.

Under the leadership of Harry Butler (who was called 'Skip' by one and all), the group continued to meet and do useful work, and by all accounts, he was almost single-handedly responsible for keeping the movement alive in Connah's Quay during the war.

During Warship Week in 1942 the boys did some fundraising for HMS *Tuscan*, making four guineas from a whist drive and they held regular dances at the Drill Hall.

When the war ended in 1945 the troop was at camp at Ellesmere, and Ken Taylor remembers the event as one of his proudest memories:

> We were in the Connah's Quay Scouts Bugle Band and marching down the street when the war finished. There was a carnival atmosphere. It was a hot day. There was me, Gordon Hannah, John Roberts and Herbie Martin on bugle, John Coppack on bass drum and Roy Hulley on side drum.

The scouts always had a good football team and one of the parents, Harold Gregory coached them. His son, Raymond, remembers how hard it was to get a decent game going locally and how the scouts ended up joining the Northop and District Football League. They called themselves Connah's Quay Juniors and played for a couple of seasons under this name until a local footballing hero, Tommy Jones, who played for Everton FC, took an interest in them and they transferred to the North Wales Coast League and changed their name again to the Nomads!

The 1st Connah's Quay Scouts Bugle Band..

The Rock n' Roll Years

After the war, when Gilbert returned home, he took over as Scout Leader. Skip became Group Scout Leader but continued to be involved with both Scouts and Wolf Cubs. Allan Roberts joined the Cubs in 1946 and remembers many winter evenings when Skip would gather the boys around the old pot-bellied stove in the hut and tell them ghost stories. With just the burning coke to give them warmth and light, it is easy to imagine how thrilling and mesmerising that must have been and to understand why Skip was held in such affection by everyone.

The Wolf Cubs based their training on Rudyard Kipling's *Jungle Book* story and they did the 'Dance of Ka' regularly where the 'snake' chased the 'monkeys' around the room. In learning how to become Cubs, the boys imagined that they really were like new cubs opening their eyes to the world. They worked towards stars. The first one looked like one eye open, the second like two. Most of the skills learned were about looking after themselves and other people, and much of it was as basic as learning how to clean shoes properly.

The 1950s was an exciting time for scouts. The decade kicked off with a concert by the scouts at St. David's Institute in Mold Road. This was the first of many entertainments and of some serious fund raising. There were beetle and whist drives, tombola and a very popular annual flower and vegetable show. Most of these events were held in the Scout Hut, but larger affairs like Old Tyme dances, concerts and gang shows were held in the Drill Hall or a church hall. One of the events in the old hut was a bingo night when the weather was exceptionally cold. The heating was going full blast when a wall caught fire from one of the two coke-burning stoves. As the tongue and groove lining went up in flames someone shouted, 'Gilbert, the wall's on fire!' The

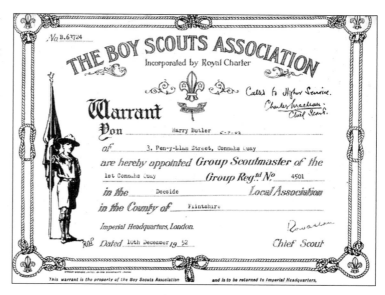

Harry Butler's Warrant.

Wolf Cub Handbook.

leaders quickly put the fire out and the people, with great stoicism, carried on playing bingo.

The Parents' Committee was very active at this time and could boast of having £100 in the bank (approximately £2,000 today)! With 128 members, the group was the largest in north Wales and flourished under the vigilant eye of Harry 'Skip' Butler. He successfully steered the scouts through the post-war years.

Scouts were not the only organisation to grow; the same thing was happening to the girls' groups. In February 1951, Skip made an appeal for more leaders in the *Buckley, Mold and Deeside Leader*:

Where are the Scouts? This was the plea from H. Butler, Scoutmaster. It is not a question of what happened to the Cubs and Brownies as what happened to their leaders.

Young girls are waiting to join but as is the case in our movement, the scouts, we are all short of leaders. There are large numbers of Brownies waiting to join but they will be disappointed. Where are the guides and scouts of yesterday? Surely the enjoyment and fellowship they had warrants a thought to help us out today. So through the medium of your paper, will you carry out a WOLF HOWL for us and do your best?

There were camps and jamborees. Transport was always provided by Jack Hannah who ran the greengrocer's store. His wagon would hold all the lads sitting on top of their equipment. In August 1950, the scouts returned to Ellesmere, this time for ten days. The *Buckley, Mold and Deeside Leader* reported:

This is the 9th time the troop have camped at this ideal site. Wednesday was parents' day when a coachload of Connah's Quay parents came to visit.

1st Connah's Quay receives the Good Camp certificate.

Festival of Britain Camp in Wepre Woods.

The Festival of Britain was celebrated by holding an all Flintshire camp in Wepre woods. The *Buckley, Mold and Deeside Leader*, 13 July 1951 reported:

On land where centuries ago, Welsh and English warriors clashed, another bugle note was sounded last weekend. Friday night saw a large area of Wepre Park covered by 30 tents in which lived 125 boy scouts drawn from 10 troops: Connah's Quay, Saltney, Hawarden, Hope, St. Asaph, Greenfield, Holywell, Hope Church, Mold and Cefn Mawr. The occasion was the Deeside Festival of Britain Patrol Camp. Present there was the North Wales Field Commissioner, John Sweet of Prestatyn, and Group Scout Master Harry Butler. Saturday morning saw the building of a suspension rope bridge over Wepre Pool. In the afternoon forestry work. The scouts felled two ash trees 45 feet high. Night camp fires and all the traditional songs. Sunday saw the serious business of inspection of patrol sites by the field commissioner. It had been preceded by a 'Scouts Own' Service and a presentation to Harry Butler for organising the event. The Scouts repaid the hospitality of Connah's Quay UDC by clearing litter from the park.

Camp site.

Harry 'Skip' Butler.

At this time Harry Butler was also presented with the prestigious 'Medal of Merit' for services to scouting generally.

Other joint events included an 'Action and Ideas Camp' at Caergwrle in 1952 which was attended by groups from Bangor, Brymbo, Cefn Mawr, Colwyn Bay, Connah's Quay, Flint, Greenfield, Hanmer, Hope, Llandudno, Llangollen, Llay Mechanics, Prestatyn, Rhyl, Ruabon, Saltney Ferry, Trevor and Wrexham. There were also jamborees in Haverfordwest, south-west Wales and Norfolk, and nearer home at Gredington Park, Hanmer. The Norfolk trip almost ended in disaster before it began; all the kit had gone ahead by road and the troop were travelling by train which was just about to pull out of Chester station when some eagle-eyed scout spotted a forgotten item of luggage sitting on the platform. It was the tin trunk containing several hundred pounds of their camp money. Fortunately, a porter came to the rescue and managed to hoist it onto the train in time!

At Gredington, the home of Lord Kenyon, 1,500 Scouts from many parts England and Wales enjoyed a ten-day World Jamboree. At this time the Chief Scout was Lord Rowallen who said that, 'The biggest job was to feed the hungry young fellows'. The *Chester Chronicle* reported:

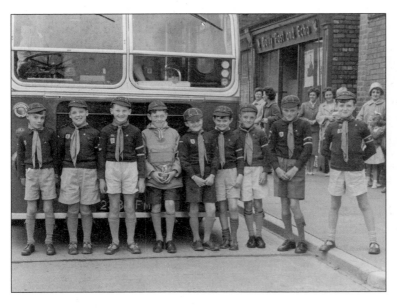

They went through 10,000 pints of milk, 5,000 loaves, 10,000 eggs, 3 tons of potatoes, 6,000 sausages, 3,000 jars of jam 12,000 rashers of bacon. There was a daily supply of fruit and vegetables and a fine tuck shop on site. The 1st Connah's Quay troop attended in the care of Gilbert Butler. They brought

Cubs setting off for camp.

with them 5 homemade canoes built with money from the collection and sale of jam jars. Each boy has contributed 3*d*. a week to funds. The canoe racing on the mere was the highlight of the Jamboree. An overseas contingent was there from Burma, Belgium, Canada, Germany, Holland, Ireland, and the USA led by James Haggart of Boulder Colarado, a very prominent figure in USA scouts.

John Butler recalls Gredington Park:

On that camp a stoat or weasel got into the stores and ate two or three loaves of bread. There was a competition with the canoes. The lads had long poles with sacking strapped to the ends. They jousted in the water! What a laugh!

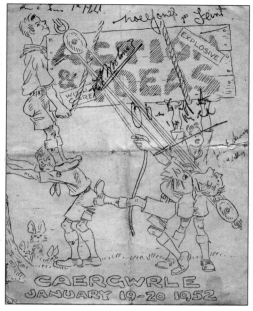

Action and Ideas camp.

The home made canoes had first been trialled at the camp at Chirk Castle where each patrol took it in turns to go off for the day on the canal. With sandwiches and pop to sustain them, they stayed out all day returning in time for the evening meal.

Camps were always on a green field site so every facility had to be fashioned from nature. Latrines were dutifully dug out but real craft was to be found in the camp kitchens that were triumphs of skill and ingenuity; the boys made wooden dressers, built fireplaces and carved utensils. Allan Roberts remembers the Trading Post where 1st Connah's Quay scouts sold items they had made from natural materials There were knives, forks, spoons and even place mats made out of wood. They were so good at this that one year they even made their own money! Those stock items, pioneering poles, were employed in many ways at home and at camp.

Scouts continued to be useful and one of the ways they did this in the community was during Bob-a -Job Week. Boys undertook a variety of tasks such as mowing lawns, chopping sticks, whitewashing cellars, clearing out lumber, litter picking, washing cars, cleaning windows, and minding babies while mothers went out shopping. This was a tradition that was not universally liked by Scout Leaders because they felt the boys were sometimes exploited. One lad spent two whole days slicing bread and putting it into packets in a bakery and was given a shilling! Another two creosoted a fence measuring 20 feet long and again received a shilling.

In the mid-fifties, the first edition of 1st Connah's Quay Scout Troop magazine was brought out. It was full of information about activities and badges. The emphasis was still on very practical matters. The Jobman Badge was popular and details of how to gain it was in one edition. A scout had to:

Paint a door
Replace a tap washer
Take up, beat and replace a carpet
Whitewash a wall
Repair a gate or fence
Oil and adjust a lawn mower
Darn a hole in a sock
Sew on a button neatly
Sharpen scissors
Attend to stopped gutters

Because scouting was so practical, it meant that the boys were far in advance of their non-scouting peers. When the Duke of Edinburgh's Award was introduced, scouts were not allowed to participate at first because many of the requirements were the same as those for the Queen's Scout. Later on, when they were allowed to try for it, their scout training enabled them to dispense with the bronze and go straight for silver.

Saturday afternoons in Wepre Park were still very popular and the troop made the most of what nature had to offer. The woods offered lots of scope for scouting activities such as rope work. Wildlife was studied and many hours were spent making plaster casts of bird tracks. The sessions always ended with the boys making a fire to boil water for tea and eating packets of sandwiches brought from home.

In 1957, to commemorate the Jubilee year of the Boy Scouts Association and the centenary of the birth of Baden-Powell, there was a programme of local celebrations beginning with a church parade at St. Mark's Church.

Above: Scouts.

Centre right: Pioneering poles.

Far right: An example of pole work.

Over 350 Scouts, Cubs, Guides and Brownies attended from Connah's Quay, Hawarden, Shotton, Mancot and the American Scouts at the RAF base in Sealand. They marched past the council yard on High Street, where they were inspected by the Lord Lieutenant of the County. There was also a week-long touring exhibition of the Boy Scout movement which was opened at the Scout HQ in Connah's Quay on Monday by Mrs Joan Scott, Chair of the UDC. The exhibition visited the new school at Saltney on Tuesday, St John's Hall at Queensferry on Wednesday, the Tithe Barn in Hawarden on Thursday, Shotton Scout HQ on Friday (where it was opened by Sir Geoffrey Summers) and finished at Broughton Institute on Saturday.

In January 1959, 1st Connah's Quay Scouts celebrated the start of its own half century year with a hotpot supper at the drill hall. As well as 120 scouts and cubs, also present were: Group Scout Leader,

DIEU ET MON DROIT

DAVID WILLIAMS

AS A QUEEN'S SCOUT you have prepared yourself for service to God and your fellowmen, and have shown yourself a worthy member of the great SCOUT BROTHERHOOD. I wish you God-speed on your journey through life; may it prove for you a joyous adventure.

Elizabeth R

Above right: Queen's Scout Certificate.

The Troop parading down from St. Mark's Church. Eyes left at the old fountain at the top of Dock Road. Among the dignitaries are Len Williams (of Connah's Quay UDC) and Mr Coppack (headmaster of Custom House Lane School).

DEESIDE BOY SCOUTS' ASSOCIATION

1957

Baden Powell

Centenary Celebrations

AND 50 YEARS OF SCOUTING

AN EXHIBITION

will be held at

Connah's Quay Headquarters ... ... Monday, 25th March
Saltney Secondary School ... ... Tuesday, 26th March
Queensferry St. John's Hall ... ... Wednesday, 27th March
Hawarden Tithebarn ... ... Thursday, 28th March
Shotton Youth Club, King George St. ... Friday, 29th March
All the above to commence at 6.30 p.m.
Broughton Institute ... ... Saturday, 30th March
To commence at 4.0 p.m.

PROGRAMME 6d.

This programme admits to Exhibition.

DEESIDE BOY SCOUTS' ASSOCIATION

1957

Baden Powell

Centenary Celebrations

AND 50 YEARS OF SCOUTING

EXHIBITS

MODEL CAMP SITE and KAYAKS ... ... 1st. Connah's Quay.
CAMP KITCHEN ... ...1st. Shotton.
BACKWOODS SHELTER ... ... 1st. Hawarden.
PIONEERING ... ... 1st. Saltney Ferry.
TENDERFOOT TO QUEEN'S SCOUT ... ... 1st. Broughton.
B-P CORNER ... ... 2nd. Saltney (St. Anthony's).

LITERATURE —— PHOTOGRAPHS —— HANDICRAFTS

Programme for the 50th Anniversary of Scouting Exhibition.

H. Butler, Scoutmaster G. Butler and 10 assistant scout leaders (7 of whom had joined as cubs) and Mr T. G. Mullett (Chair of local Boy Scout Association). Guests included the vicar, Mrs Eirene White MP, Mr Les Coppack (Chair of Connah's Quay UDC), Major Seymour Thomas and Mr and Mrs Peter D'Eath. The hotpot was cooked by Mrs Butler and served by lady members of the Parents' Committee. A birthday cake decorated with the Scout Badge was distributed to all present. There were speeches by S. Thomas on the Scout movement in general, by Scoutmaster Butler on Scouting in Connah's Quay and by Mr Les Coppack on 'Scouting and Citizenship'.

In February, a Scouts' Own Service was held at St. Mark's Church preceded by a parade from the Scout HQ in Chapel Street. There were many visiting troops and a march past at which the salute was taken by Lord Kenyon, the Commissioner for Wales. Refreshments afterwards were in the Scout Hut. The St. George's Day service that year was at St Mark's. There were 400 Boy Scouts, Wolf Cubs and Girl Guides from Connah's Quay, Queensferry,

THE BOY SCOUTS ASSOCIATION
BADEN-POWELL MEMORIAL FUND

25 BUCKINGHAM PALACE ROAD, LONDON, S.W.1.
Telephone : VICtoria 6005.

W.G.H.Butler, Esq.,
64, Dee Road,
Connah's Quay,
Nr. Chester.

17th March, 1959.

Dear Mr. Butler,

It was most generous of your Group to donate to the Memorial Fund the collections taken at your film show and Thanksgiving Service. We appreciate this very much indeed and perhaps you would pass on our thanks to the Group.

The Group is to be congratulated on its 50th Anniversary and I hope it will go from strength to strength.

With many thanks for your support and interest.

Yours sincerely,

Roy A. Shapley

Organising Secretary.

Letter from Baden-Powell House.

Hawarden, Sandycroft and Saltney. The parade assembled at the Connah's Quay UDC office headed by the Deva Sea Cadets band from Chester.

At this time, there was a general plea for Scout groups all over the UK to contribute to the building of Baden-Powell House in Kensington, and 1st Connah's Quay scouts contributed regularly, collecting money in a little cardboard box shaped like a

Taking the salute outside Connah's Quay UDC.

brick. The group was entered in the Roll of House-Founder Groups and had brick N⁰. 595.

1st Connah's Quay seemed to be going from strength to strength and the enthusiasm of the boys was excellent. There were fifteen Queen's Scout Awards given to the troop during the 1950s, but there was still the perennial problem of attracting leaders.

At the 1959 AGM of the Parents' Committee, there was a plea for more scouters to assist in the training of boys. Gilbert spoke of that year's camp at Maerdy, Corwen, which was the best and driest camp he had ever known.

All together. The full group.

To finish off the 50th anniversary celebrations about 100 children and adults attended a Guy Fawkes display at the old clay hole recreation ground. The Rotary Club and Round Table had erected nine field kitchens serving hot dogs and other hot refreshments were provided by the Boy Scouts Association, Connah's Quay UDC and the local committee of World Refugee Year.

Cubs at camp. Boys wear their ordinary clothes most of the time at camp. Keeping their uniform smart for travelling in and for ceremonies.

Changing times — the '60s and '70s

The pre-war plans for a new Scout HQ were resurrected in the fifties, and the group was given a plot of land on which to build a new Hut on the disused clay pit just over the road from the old tin building. The truth was that the Council had decided to landscape the whole area and the old tin hut with its various extensions was a bit of an eyesore. They decided that it had to go. On 12 March 1960, the chair of the Council, Ivor Cotterill, cut the first piece of turf from the ground for the new HQ. At the ceremony, J. W. Coppack said that he was the only survivor of the original Scout Committee of fifty years ago. He said:

> They used to boast that they were the 1st troop in North Wales but it was proved that someone had beaten them to it by a few hours. I well remember when we had only 6 boys and the troop often had nowhere to meet except in stables and disused shops. The troop now numbers 123.

Permission was granted by Connah's Quay UDC for the Scouts to have a house-to-house collection and £500 was raised for the new headquarters. But that, of course, was not enough. First of all, Gilbert visited the home of every boy in the group and asked for assistance from bricklayers, joiners and anyone who could use a shovel. They worked by paraffin light until 10 o'clock at night. John Butler remembers re-using bricks and chipping cement off the old ones in the February frost. John Summers' Steel Works provided much of the materials for the frame of the building, and Mrs Summers personally arranged and paid for £250 worth of bricks to be delivered from the Castle Brick Works.

The purlins came from Summers, but the electrics, the roof and the paint, had to be bought in from Ellesmere Port. However, Gilbert himself made all the door frames. He would come home after the 6am–2pm shift at John Summers, have a bit of dinner, then go straight down to the site to work for another seven hours, every day of the week. He remembers:

The old tin hut, meeting place for the Scout group.

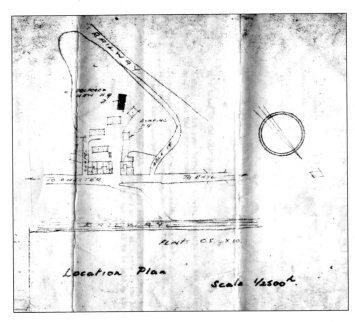

Plan of the area for the new Scout Hut.

There were five dedicated brick-layers who were in the habit of ambling down at some point in the afternoon. By about 6pm they would get a bit of a thirst on whereupon two enamel jugs would be taken down to the Hare and Hounds Public House and the landlord would bring them back full to the brim. The brickies were great lads but thirsty!

Eric Parry, the Assistant County Commissioner, wrote to Lord Kenyon about the frenzy of activity going on in Connah's Quay:

I am not sure how much you may know about the new 1st Connah's Quay HQ (close by their existing one). It represents one of the outstanding examples of effort and co-operation between parents, local industry and local government officers. A magnificent building (contract quoted price was £4,500) it has been erected by 95% voluntary labour, advice and assistance. It makes a remarkable story. Work progresses amazingly well and the final stages (ceiling, floor, heating) have been reached. John Summers have been truly wonderful and Mrs Summers is to open the HQ in April.

Eventually it was all done bar the painting, and Gilbert told the lads to go home for the weekend and painted it himself, giving it several coats. The committee had vowed that they would do the job of building a new headquarters for £1,000 but they overspent by £28 which was the cost of hiring the marquee for the opening ceremony. Also they did not anticipate the plasterer's bill, but Gilbert sold his car to pay for that and went to work on his bike.

So, with a great deal of help and support, the new Scout Hut was built within twelve months. Sir Richard and Lady Summers officially opened the building which was most fitting since they had been so supportive. It was said that if the hut could walk, it would walk all the way back to Summers!

The Building Committee were all present at the opening and there was a dedication and presentation by the Rev. Boyer. Afterwards, there were sandwiches and a buffet, the older scouts had a disco in the hut and the elderly folk repaired to the Old Quay House. In the newspaper report of the opening of new HQ, J. W. Coppack recalled how:

Turf cutting ceremony. Ivor Cotterill cuts the first piece.

Building the new Scout HQ.

One of the builders sets the dedication stone in place.

Above right: 'Skip' unveils the dedication stone.

The opening ceremony with Lady Summers.

The late E. Ll. Marriott personally received from Baden-Powell the charter which he hung in the hut with great pride and ceremony. Founded in 1909, it was one of the oldest troops in the country.

The new building was wonderful and vastly different from the old tin hut. The committee was determined that it would be looked after and treated with respect. This was hard to achieve given the physical nature of scouting but precautions were taken to protect it. Inside the hut, metal guards were fitted to the lights to prevent damage during games. The boys complained that it was too much like a palace because they were banned from walking on the new Marley-tiled floor in their boots; they had to wear pumps instead. Also, presumably for the adults using the building, ashtrays were needed to clip onto the backs of chairs in the hall and a list of rules was pinned up.

> Litter bin to be used at all times.
> Floor to be kept clean.
> No bullying by elder lads either outside or inside the
>   building. Drastic action will be taken if caught.
> Chairs not to be misused by treading on them.
> No writing on the toilet walls.
> Whispering on parade to be stopped immediately.

However, the new HQ soon needed extending. There were plans to renovate the old trek cart — a new axle shaft was required, and the wheels needed to be re-tyred. Generally there were problems about storing gear. It was decided to buy ex-British Rail horse-boxes for this purpose, but permission was refused. Eventually the Old Mortuary in Cable Street became available in 1975 and was leased from Alyn and Deeside District Council. The Scouts had the storage they desperately needed and, even though they had to store their kit in body drawers, they did not mind. Scouts are made of stern stuff and are never squeamish!

In 1961, the *Scout Yearbook* paid tribute to 1st Connah's Quay for producing two Queen's Scouts, Raymond Wynne and Graham Hughes. They were congratulated on supporting and preparing them on top of a full troop programme. A testimonial fund was opened for Skip Butler and there followed a programme of fundraising events including the Annual Fruit and Vegetable Show which was very well

Parents Committee keep the new HQ spick and span.

'Skip' with the lads.

attended. Local gardeners worked towards it throughout the growing season and competition was fierce. Gordon Henshaw recalls it being a 'very good fundraiser'.

It cost only 3*d*. or 6*d*. to enter the exhibits and the winners received prizes of 5*s*. but the main thing was the auction of all the produce a wonderful way of raising money. The marquee was set up outside … it was a big hefty one, old army surplus. A real beauty to put up … the problem was taking it down … when everyone had gone home!

There was no shortage of ideas for activities, including pantomimes and gang shows. It was suggested that the group should borrow the old Alhambra picture house equipment, now in the possession of Deeside Cinema, and apply to the Tivoli in Buckley for some curtains. Fêtes were held and the side shows included football, cricket, a slow bicycle race, golf, darts, a coconut shy, tin cans, judo demonstrations, Morris Dancers, trampoline and the gymnastics team from Aston School. The Parents' Committee also decided

Harvest Festival.

Senior Scouts.

that the outside of the Scout Hut needed re-decorating with flower boxes, and trees were planted after the Council had completed the playing field. There was a football team and matches were arranged with the Boy's Brigade and the Army Cadets. With so much business to attend to, it is small wonder that the Parents' Committee decided to hold their annual dinner at the Custom House Hotel instead of catering for themselves. Impressed with the success of the Scout Fête, Connah's Quay OAP Club and St Mark's Church asked for help with their own fêtes the following year, borrowing white tents, the marquee and stall equipment.

It was not just during recreational and fundraising activities that the group interacted with the local community; charitable work also played a large part. There was the annual Harvest Festival where the lads collected fruit for children, and vegetables for the elderly, and each Christmas, as part of their 'Good Turns', bags of firewood were distributed to OAPs. There were also schemes of a more serious nature, such as the idea of providing training for boys on probation. This was suggested to the police in 1961, but not implemented.

The boys continued going to camp and John Butler recalls that:

We always found a site where there was a field, river, hedge and a church. We would go to church on Sunday and once the vicar came by afterwards and saw Wilson tickling trout; he ended up taking one home! We usually went to a farm, and not a registered scout site. There would be a plentiful supply of milk and vegetables and if we went in August, we helped with the harvest and got these free of charge. We were always allowed to go down and dig up spuds as required and I always remember leaving one farm where the farmer gave each boy a fresh chicken to take home because they had helped with the corn harvest and sheep dipping as well. The wettest camp was at Llangollen when we had to sleep in a barn, and the hottest was at Overton where we had more than 80 boys and it was so hot they had to wear their pyjama bottoms underneath their shorts to stop their legs getting sunburned.

The early 1960s saw the formation of a Senior Troop which expanded the activities of the group. These older boys took their scouting further afield and had regular rock climbing weekends and trips to Snowdonia. A Friendship Club was formed, and a guitar group was engaged for the first social where only Coke and crisps were on sale! More daringly, a Norton motorbike was acquired which was taxed and insured for the Senior Scouts but this was short-lived after OAPs living nearby complained about the noise!

Cubs at camp.

Above: Cubs at camp with Wilson Prydderch.

The Scout group attends all Civic Ceremonies. Here they are marching down Wepre Drive in Connah's Quay.

Cubs outside their tent at camp.

The ideal camp site.

Catching supper.

After a full day's activities there is no time to change into uniform for the flag ceremony.

The local newspapers covered some of the activities:

The recently formed Senior troop of 1st CQ Boy Scouts held their annual party at the HQ. A large number attended this being symbolic of the revived interest in Senior Scouting. Guides and Rangers from other parts of the District were guests of the boys. Also present were Senior Scout Master, Mr Harvey Lloyd and his assistant Mr John Williams. The chicken salad meal was prepared by the boys themselves. Dancing to records followed and the MC was Mr Peter Castrey, aided by Mr Raymond Wynne.

In 1963, the Chief Commissioner for Wales, Lord Kenyon organised a Senior Scout camp at Gwersyll Bryniau which was attended by people from all over the UK, Germany and Holland. Some travelled in small groups, others by themselves. One of these Lone Scouts was Derek Shelmerdine from 1st Connah's Quay.

In 1965 a story of great bravery hit the headlines when Harvey Lloyd and John Williams, who were mountaineering in Snowdonia, dived into a river and saved a girl from drowning.

At home the group began putting together a library of books about Scouting which were to be issued to Scouters only, but there was no bookcase to keep them in. It was decided to apply to local furniture stores, Moreton Green or Brown's for one. Local businesses, both large and small, had traditionally always been very generous to the group; from John Summers' building assistance, to Jack Hannah's lorry for camp, the most recent patron was the Deeside Power Station which had provided heaters for the building. The library was very dear to the heart of Skip Butler and after his death, Ivor Cotterill, chairman of the Council, spoke of this and of the decision to purchase a reference library of Scouting books as a lasting memento and in recognition of his good work in Connah's Quay and Deeside.

Setting off to the plains of Marathon, Greece for the World Jamboree.

A second Wolf Cub pack was formed in 1963. The two packs were called Mohawks and Cherokees. At one stage, due to a shortage of adult help, the Cherokees merged with the Mohawks for a time but in 1971, the Scout Leader at the time, Richard Peers asked two of the ACSLs, Christine Burdock and Ann McFerran to re-open the Cherokees. The Mohawks continued under the leadership of Ian Matthews, who was in charge for many years. When he eventually left, the name changed to the Dakotas for a few years before reverting to the Mohawks. In those days, summer camps were still quite long. Sometimes the Scouts would go for the first week and leave everything set up for the Cubs, who would arrive for the second week. Thus the workload was halved. The Mohawks were in the habit of having an extra long camp every third year, when they would go as far as Scotland or south Wales. The group still went to Plas Bellin for short weekend camps and it was at one of these that Ian Matthews remembers Wilson Prydderch telling the boys late one night to race to the end of the field where a red lamp was shining. The first one to reach it and bring it back was promised a prize. It was something of a mystery as it disappeared before anyone had the chance to reach it. The red lamp

turned out to be the light on top of Connah's Quay Power station down by the river! The Senior Scouts had the use of a small cottage in the woods at Northop Hall for local activities, but they would camp out or stay in hostels when they went on longer expeditions.

Senior Scouts out and about.

Senior Scout Badges.

Poster for the London Excursion train.

Brian Jones with the Cub pack. Lord Kenyon looking on.

National Scout Centre at Gilwell.

In 1974, the annual St. George's Day Parade was held at the Deeside Leisure Centre. Guides and Brownies attended and Father Shepherd from the Roman Catholic church officiated.

In April 1977, the very first issue of the group newsletter, *Quaynotes,* was produced which helped to keep people informed about what was going on. In 1979, Dave Rowlands reported that a Venture Scout Group would open in Connah's Quay.

By the end of the seventies, a new fund had been set up to build an extension to the Scout Headquarters. Everyone got involved and one of the most ambitious projects to raise money was a day excursion to London by train organised by Dave Rowlands. The whole group went with their families in tow, and a jolly good time was had by all. Once again, the Steelworks supported Scouts with a generous donation from the Julian Melchett Trust.

During this period there were several trips to Gilwell National Scouting Centre.

Parading along High Street Connah's Quay.

Members of the group receive a cheque from the Steelworks Julian Melchett Trust.

Above left: Airing the tents.

Above: Inspection at camp by the Chief Scout, Lord Maclean.

Flag ceremony at camp.

Expansion — the '80s and '90s

The 1980s were a time of expansion generally. For the Parents' Committee in particular, there was an intense calendar of fund-raising activities that were so popular they are still talked of today with nostalgia. The Spring Fayre, the Rounders Match and Barbecue in the summer, the Cub Football Tournament, sponsored walks, treasure hunts, race nights, cheese and wine evenings, a nearly-new family auction, the Autumn Fayre and Flower Show and Easter Bingo. At Christmas there was an abundance of events: the Carol Service, the Turkey Bingo, the Christmas Dance, the Grand Raffle, the Christmas Fayre (with Santa's Grotto) and the annual Get-Together which took places in venues like Highfield Hall. For several years the group took part in the Deeside Festival, sometimes running stalls or entering a float in the carnival and always organising the car parking on Wepre Fun Day. This was a real money-spinner.

The group continued to take part in activities further afield. In 1982, nineteen Cherokee Cubs attended the camp at Cal Dol Park which was highlighted by a visit from the Chief Scout, and they excelled in the Cub Scout District Hike. A special train took Cubs from north Wales to the Royal

Cub football.

Cherokee Cubs.

65

Cubs cooking to gain their Cooking Badge.

Welsh Agricultural Showground at Builth Wells for the Cub Fun Day and to the County Camp at Leeswood where Connah's Quay won the competition and also came 2nd and 3rd in the District cooking competition.

1st Connah's Quay Scout Group had always had an ambivalent attitude towards its own age and this has been reflected in the dates chosen to celebrate the milestones throughout the century. The fiftieth anniversary used 1909 as the start date but the seventy fifth and ninetieth counted from 1908. At the 75th anniversary there was a service at St. Mark's and a parade from the Kwiksave car park on the High Street through Connah's Quay. Afterwards there were light refreshments served at the Scout Hut. On April 17th a Celebration Dance was held at the Civic Hall. Opinion is still divided today about whether the group was founded in 1908 or 1909.

The Boys' Brigade Unit started in Connah's Quay in 1984 and large numbers of boys left the Scouts to join. Throughout the century, the numbers had fluctuated a great deal. At the Scout group's AGM that year, Mr Brian Unwin, headteacher of Connah's Quay High School, was the guest speaker and he spoke of how interesting it was that scouting had survived for such an enormously long time. He attributed it to the fact that at its heart, scouting has some very important ideas and at the same time has managed to change with the times.

The Scout building was extended with the addition of a large storeroom and two extra rooms and this, like the main building, was built by the voluntary labour of members of the group.

Plans for extension to the Scout Hut.

Alan Henshaw and the extension.

Leaders and helpers build the extension.

There were a number of changes and improvements generally to the rest of the building: gas heating was installed and the cold tiles in the hall were replaced with a wooden floor, much to the delight of the cubs who could now play crab football without freezing their nether regions. A suggestion was made that the room at the north end of the extension be called the Marriott Room and a portrait of the founder hangs in there to this day.

From its inception, Cubs has always been strong in Connah's Quay and there has been a long waiting list to join one of the two packs for many years. Mark Sephton joined Cubs in 1986 and remembers wearing his own clothes for the 4–6 week initial settling-in period, learning about the *Jungle Book* theme and eventually taking part in hikes, parades and glorious camps where they cooked on an open fire, made a clay oven and had 'wide' games in the woods. As a Scout he remembers the fundraising that is always a part of scouting, car washing and the Christmas Fayre with Santa's Grotto. This magical creation was always organised by the Venture Scouts.

In 1986, younger boys from the age of six were allowed to join the movement by the establishment of Beaver Scouts. Connah's Quay got its own Beaver Colony started by Christine Roberts. The very first boys to be invested were Neil Roberts, Paul Simon, Daniel Morris and Joshua Evans. Of all the sections, this one has perhaps always been the most consistent. It is always full, and always has a waiting list. Christine had previously run Cherokees before her marriage. Her son, Neil, was the first Beaver to be invested and today he holds the record for having belonged to every section of the group. He moved up to Cubs, Scouts, Venture Scouts and is today Assistant Scout Leader.

Cubs and leaders.

Tessa Christian with the Cherokee Cubs.

Left: Cherokees.

Roy Christan and the Cherokees.

In the mid eighties the group had good numbers; thirty Scouts, thirty-six Cubs in each pack and twenty-four Beavers.

Despite this, the shortage of leaders was so acute that for the first time in seventy-five years there was no Scout camp in 1987. At the beginning of the nineties, numbers were still good with 132 on the roll in all sections.

The last decade of the century began with a tribute to Gilbert Butler. He had already received the Silver Wolf, the highest award for services to scouting in 1981, but in January 1990 Connah's Quay Town Council celebrated his work with a presentation for services to the community. Gilbert was the driving force behind the fundraising and the building of the Headquarters at Connah's Quay and also the Gladstone Centre at Hawarden. At the ceremony he said:

Scouting is a brotherhood of friendship and it widens boys' minds. You meet a lot of people. I have friends all over the country.

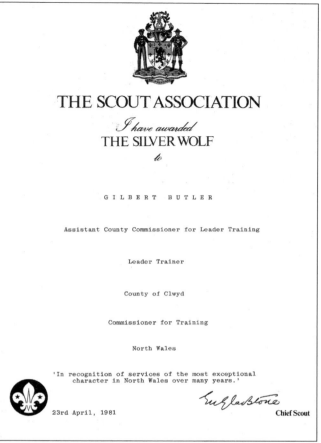

Gilbert Butler's Silver Wolf Award, presented at Windsor.

Safety and first aid have always been part of badge work in the Scout movement but one of the Cub groups took their skills to new heights during the nineties. Trained by ACSL Steve Thomas, Mohawks represented Deeside four times at the National First Aid Competition in Torquay, Derby, Cardiff and Salisbury and in 1997 the event was hosted in Connah's Quay.

Finding the money for the upkeep of the Scout Hut continued as always, but the calendar of events gradually dwindled as tastes changed and new ventures were tried such as car boot sales and a Fifty Club. By the end of the decade only the Turkey Bingo Nights remained as fundraising social occasions for the group.

Still working on 1908 as the start date, the highlight of the nineties was the big event to celebrate ninety years of scouting in Connah's Quay. A family camp was held at Pontblyddyn in 1998. Over 150 people spent a wonderful weekend in a farmer's field and although it drizzled with rain, it did not dampen anyone's spirits. Graham Roberts was the camp cook and his mess

Ian Matthews with the Mohawk Cubs.

tent was a marvel to behold. The last day was a celebration of all the years that had gone before and old photographs were spread out on tables in the marquee. These were pored over by young and old alike and the numbers swelled during the afternoon as many more people turned up. As dusk fell everyone started to move towards the camp fire and those who owned them wore their camp blankets embellished with badges and pennants from other camps, jamborees and from a shared past. It was an enormous circle of scouting family and friends and the singing and sketches went on for a very long time until the embers died away.

Into the 21st Century

1st Connah's Quay has always been a very traditional group because of the continuity from one generation to the next and the involvement of so many key families. Many of the members today, both leaders and boys, come from a long line of scouts and methods of scouting have been passed on and exist quite happily alongside new rules and innovations. Much of the equipment was certainly used by the first scoutmasters. It is only within the last five years that the old heavy pre-war tents have been replaced by newer nylon ones. And the lads miss the old ones …

for one thing there is no nice stout pole to hang onto when you are putting your wellies on! But there are echoes of the past to be found in the games, campfire songs and woodcraft still practised by today's scouts.

Campfire singing led by Allan Roberts.

These old ways co-exist happily with new ones and modern scouts are given every opportunity to acquire new skills.

1st Connah's Quay is probably one of the last bastions where the old tradition known as 'going over the poles' is still kept up. This is when a boy moves on from Cubs to Scouts. He climbs over two long pioneer poles held at waist and shoulder height by his Cub leaders and leaps from the top one where he is greeted on the other side by the Scout leader. This ceremony is very exciting and looked forward to by all the boys. It symbolises the new challenges ahead in Scouts.

Scouting has most definitely changed. Indeed how could it not, during the course of 100 years? However, although there are the inevitable grumbles about red tape and bureaucracy, there remains at the heart of the most modern and well-informed scout more than a smidgen of that old B-P spirit. It is undoubtedly at the core of every member of this wonderful movement which has evolved and survived from the nineteenth century siege of Mafeking into the twenty-

Dedication Ceremony at Bryn Road Cemetery 4 March 2006. The Rev Paul Varah officiated.

first century. The reason for this cannot properly be explained so we must simply accept that 'the marvellous invention of the Boy Scout Movement' by Lord Baden-Powell, must indeed be utterly brilliant.

The 1st Connah's Quay Scout Troop hooked into their past in a very special way on 4 March 2006 when they remembered their founder, Captain Marriott, by marking his grave with a simple wooden cross, sixty-four years after his death. Perhaps because he had no children, and maybe because he died during the Second World War, his grave was unmarked except for the metal tag that bore the reference, Y28.

As part of the Centenary Project, two former scouts, Peter Hutton and Harvey Lloyd, made the cross, had a brass plaque inscribed and organised a dedication ceremony which was conducted by the Rev. Paul Varah. It was on a clear March morning, made all the brighter by a thick layer of snow covering the ground that a good crowd gathered in Connah's Quay Cemetery for a long overdue acknowledgement of a scouting hero.

So almost 100 years after Captain Marriott found out about scouting for boys, today's scouts saluted him and give him a memorial for the past, for the present and for all who come after them in the future. They gave public recognition to the dedication of the founder of Connah's Quay Scouts by a man who adopted the town as his own and served its people well. A true Scout.

Going over the poles.

Cubs abseiling at Ashworth Camp

On the climbing wall.

The water slide, always a favourite.

Waiting to ascend.

Around the camp fire.

Cubs being checked before ascending the climbing wall.

In conclusion

Pat Wilson (Chair of the Centenary Committee)

Three cheers for the far-sighted gentleman who introduced Scouting to Connah's Quay, Lt. Commander Edward Llewellyn Marriott, known to the scouts as Captain Marriott.

Following in Captain Marriott's footsteps have been many Group Scout Leaders, Assistant Scout Leaders, Akelas, Assistant Cub Scout Leaders and twenty years ago we expanded the group with a Beaver Leader.

All these leaders were warranted but we also had helpers – Mums and Dads who came to meetings, served on the committee, organised events, sales etc. raised money for the maintenance of the HQ and were dedicated to keeping Scouting on the map.

Having been associated with Scouting for thirty five years as Scouter and committee member, I say, 'Let's be prepared' for the next 100 years and B.R.A.V.O. for our founder, Captain Marriott.

Cherokee Cubs, 2007.

Scouts and Explorer Scouts, 2007.

Scout Wisdom

These are just a few of the comments made by people in the course of this project.

What is Scouts all about?
A Scout is trusty, loyal and helpful, courteous, kind, brotherly, smiling, thrifty, pure and obedient in body and mind.
Scouting is about making friends with like-minded fellows.
Scouting is about outdoors, learning and fun.
You try to respect other people and property and respect yourself in general.
Treat others as you'd like to be treated yourself.
Patrol leaders lead by example.
The patrols were called Peewit, Hawks, Hounds and Bulldogs.

Why you would join Scouts?
Boys enjoyed scouting for fun, friendship and adventure.
Enjoyed outdoor activities.
It had a good football team.
You learn knotting, mapping,camping,a bit of cooking and the confidence to travel the world.

On Discipline
We didn't think of it as discipline … we got discipline at home and at school. Scouts was just a good laugh.
In the past there was more discipline, but it didn't spoil the enjoyment.

On Going to Camp
You go to camp for a good laugh … you still remember even now, many a laugh.
You get to leave your parents for the first time.
For some boys going to camp was the only holiday they got.
You get to enjoy yourselves..if it gets too serious, what's the point?
Camp fire was always on the last night of camp and everyone made a big effort with songs and sketches, the dafter, the better. You didn't worry about making yourself look a fool.
Leaders should always have a look at a potential camp site in February and see the ground at its worst to check for flooding etc.

On Jamborees
Its nothing like any camp you've ever been to.
Recommend it. Experience of a lifetime. Different languages and cultures presented no problem.

The best thing were all the different badges and the badge swapping.

Opportunity to meet people from different countries.

No better way to get to know what's going on around the world.

On Bullying

It did happen in Scouts but was always dealt with right away.

If a boy was found out to be bullying, he was put into another patrol.

If a Patrol Leader was found to be bullying, his stripes were taken away from him.

The best form of control was verbal. Stand in front and wag a finger. The boy couldn't take it.

Embarrassed to be a Scout

Its nothing new. Boys used to get their legs pulled (not literally) when they walked over the Quay Hill in their short trousers.

Leaders would get ribbed when they took their uniform into work so they could go straight to the Scout Hut.

Some of the most famous people in the world are Scouts.

Proudest Memories

Getting a proper uniform with hat, shirt and staff … a proper Scout.

Seeing my parents meet the Queen because of their work with Scouts.

Making my promise.

Worst Memories

First district meeting at Shire Hall where we talked for a long time and didn't get very far and comparing that to the camaraderie of night talking round the pot-bellied stove in the old tin hut.

As a Cub finding a mouse in my welly at camp.

The night cows got into the field at camp and tripped over the tent ropes.

Travelling by train to Pembroke Jamboree and having to sleep on a luggage rack.

The marquee collapsing on top of everyone at camp due to severe flooding and having to dig a trench to divert the water before hauling it back into position.

On Former Scouts

There's a little bond because you've known each for many years and had good times together.

On how Scouting has Changed

Subs used to be 1*d*. a week.

It's the same in a lot of ways but its new rules cramp your style nowadays.

There were ten laws, now there are seven but B-P had all the right ideas.

In the old days you could tell the lads to meet on a Friday night and bring a rasher of bacon, a chop and an an egg and go off to camp for the weekend. You can't do that now … nothing's that simple and there are too many forms to fill in.

What does it Mean to be a Scout

A great honour.

A different way of life.

Scouting is a vital part of my life … the law and the promise.

Always remember your promise, always remember being invested.
The Scout Law means a lot. A Scout is to be trusted. It's a way of living.

On Joining Scouts
I'd advise people to join and try it, that's the test.
Give it a try and enjoy it. A lot of fun can be had out of scouts.
You've got to put effort in to get fun out of it.
Join … definitely. You'll get a lot out of it. Meet new people and learn new skills.
If you're going to do anything, do it right, do it properly and everyone's happy.
Do it. There's nothing better for learning skills and being presented with opportunities.

Hope for the Future
Hope that this scout unit keeps going and the lads get out in the fresh air.
If scouting went back to how it was, it would attract more boys.

Group of Scouts just about ready to set off on a trip to Skye in Scotland in the 1960s.

Appendices

1. 1ST CONNAH'S QUAY TROOP ANNUAL CAMP ELLESMERE 1949

Red Patrol Log Book   K. Evans, P. L., R. Parker, 2nd, B. Parry, M. John, D. Fewster, B. Roberts, M. Bell.

Monday 8 August: Set up camp early afternoon. Formed kitchen and set up our tent in front of it.
Tea: Bread, butter, jam & tea.
After we tidied the campsite and made gadgets etc. Then we went into Ellesmere for the evening.
Supper: Bread, butter, paste & cocoa. We turned in at approx. 11pm.

Tuesday 9th: Appointed officers for the day: cooks — B. Parry & D. Fewster; wood & water — R. Parker & M. Bell; fatigues — M. John & B. Roberts.
The cooks rose at 7.30am to light the fire. The wood & water party rose at 7.45am and performed their duties. The tent was tidied by the fatigue party whilst breakfast was being cooked.
Breakfast: Puffed wheat & milk, fried tomatoes, bread & tea.
After breakfast the dixies were cleaned and filled with water. The wood party formed a decent wood pile and the fatigue party peeled the spuds and put them on for dinner. The camp site was then cleaned and put in order.
Dinner: We had rather an early dinner at 12.30 consisting of potatoes and stew followed by a custard pudding.
We were allowed the afternoon free so we went to play the 1st Ellesmere troop at football; we drew 6–6. We then went for a dip in the mere to cool off. Returned to camp at 6pm.
Tea: Bread, butter, jam & tea.
After tea we set up a bivouac for food. When this was finished and the rations transferred from the tent, it was time to prepare supper.
Supper: Re-heated some stew left over from dinner & cocoa. Turned in at approx. 10.30pm.

Wednesday 10th: Appointed officers for the day: cooks — R. Parker & M. Bell; wood & water — M. John & B. Roberts; fatigues — D. Fewster & B. Parry.
As it was to be visitors day we were very busy so we all rose at 7.30am and started work.
Breakfast: We had an excellent breakfast of porridge, bacon, sausage meat, bread & tea. This meal was a credit to the cooks.
After breakfast we dug a new pit and filled in the old one. We also dug a pit and filled it with water to keep the milk bottles in. We attended flag break and I was on flag duty. We were given

a menu for the meals of the day.

Dinner: We had a good dinner of potatoes, meat and soup followed by apple dumpling and custard (excellent). The visitors arrived after dinner and when the dishes were washed we were free for the afternoon. Most of us went to Ellesmere with our parents.

B. Roberts changed to Blue Patrol and we had A. Fewster in exchange.

Tea: For tea we had prunes, custard, bread, jam & tea. After tea we washed up and the senior scouts were allowed to attend a social in Ellesmere (very good). The juniors also went to town but returned earlier.

Mohawk Cubs 2007.

Supper: The juniors had soup (warmed from dinner) & cocoa. The seniors returning later had nothing (too tired) Juniors turned in at 10.15pm. Seniors at 11.30pm.

Thursday 11th: Appointed officers for the day: cooks — M. John & A. Fewster; wood & water — D. Fewster & B. Parry; fatigues — R. Parker & M. Bell.

We rose at 8am this morning and tidied tent and campsite before breakfast.

Breakfast: Porridge (slightly burned) followed by eggs, tomatoes & fried bread. There was a good wood pile formed before breakfast.

Dinner: Potatoes, soup, & bread followed by stewed rhubarb.There was another exchange today when B. Parry went to Blue Patrol and we had A. Coppack instead.

We had a few girl visitors after dinner so consequently stayed in, but there was no work done.

Tea: There were some very good dampers followed by bread, butter, jam & tea. After tea we stayed in and practised camp-fire stunts & songs for the camp- fire on Friday night. Afterwards there was band practice.

Supper: We had bread & jam, bread & dripping followed by cocoa. The Blue Patrol was disbanded tonight & we have two extras tomorrow in J. Butler & B. Casey. As J. Butler was the P.L. he will share duties with me in future. We retired at approx. 10.30pm.

Friday 12th: The last whole day in camp.

Appointed officers for the day: cooks — R. Parker, D. Fewster & A. Coppack; wood & water — M. Bell & B. Casey; fatigues — M. John & A. Fewster.

We rose at 8am, tidied campsite and prepared breakfast.

Breakfast: Shredded Wheat, milk, beans, bread & coffee. After breakfast most of the patrol set out to collect wood for the camp-fire. We decided to prepare an early dinner. It was ready by 11.30am.

Dinner: potatoes, stew & bread followed by stewed rhubarb & custard. After dinner we went to the mere to swim and then to town to finish our shopping. Arrived back in camp by 5pm.

Tea: we had a communal tea in the big kitchen consisting of bread, jam & tea. After tea we finished building the camp fire.

The campfire was lit at 8.30pm. There was a good crowd of visitors and it was quite an entertaining evening. Skip was presented with a wallet on behalf of the troop.
Supper: we had bread, paste & cocoa from the big kitchen. We turned in at midnight.

Saturday 13th: There were no cooks appointed for the day as there was only breakfast to cook.
Breakfast: Weetabix, fried bread, bacon & tea. After breakfast we started to pack up our kitchen.
We tidied the site, took down the bivouac and filled in the fire and pits. We cleaned all the dixies & returned them to the main kitchen. We took down the tent just before dinner.
Dinner: potatoes and stew (made in main kitchen) After dinner we helped in taking down the big kitchen and all the cub tents. We washed and dressed ready for going home.
The lorry was about an hour late and we departed about 3.30pm. Arrived home at 5pm.
Signed: Ken Evans, Patrol Leader.

On the move with the trek cart

2. CHRONOLOGY

1903	E. Ll. Marriott moved to Connah's Quay.
1908/9	E. Ll. Marriot started the Boy Scout Troop in Connah's Quay.
1910	Troop inspected by B-P in Hawarden.
1910	Reading room lent to Marriott for the boys' use.
1911	Week-long exhibition held for Scout Troop in Connah's Quay.
1911	New Boy Scout Room opened at Dock Road.
1914	Camped at Highfield Hall and Wepre Woods.
1915	First military funeral held in Connah's Quay. Former scout.
1919	E. Ll. Marriott retires from Naval Service.
1919	Scout HQ took over registration from local associations.
1924	Scouts Rally at Queensferry.
1924	Marriott in charge of Flintshire Scouts at Wembley Jamboree.
1928	Marriott awarded Medal of Merit by Baden-Powell at Hawarden Castle.
1929	All troops re-register with Gilwell and given new number.
1930	Scouts move to new Scout Hut near clay pit.
1938	Wolf Cub Pack starts in Connah's Quay.
1942	Captain Marriott dies aged 87.
1951	Festival of Britain Camp at Wepre Park.
1952	Scout Camp Welsh Jamboree at Haverfordwest.
1956	Scouts went to Welsh Jamboree at Gredington.
1957	50th anniversary of scouting celebrated.
1957	Graham Hughes represents the group in Iceland for the 50th anniversary .
1957	Welsh Jamboree at Sutton Coldfield (Gilbert Butler Scout Leader & Allan Roberts as Patrol Leader of the Welsh Troop).
1958	Group went to Senoe Park International Jamboree, East Anglia.
1959	1st Connah's Quay celebrates own 50th anniversary.
1959	Gang Show and Hotpot Supper held in the old HQ.
1960	Work began on new HQ.
1960	Scouts Camp at Norfolk Jamboree.
1961	New HQ opened by Sir Richard and Lady Summers.
1961	Raymond Wynne, Queen's Scout accepted for America.
1962	Coach trip to Gilwell.
1962	J. Butler and A. Roberts gained Wood badge.
1962	Harry ('Skip') Butler passed away.
1963	Gilbert Butler becomes G.S.M .
1963	Second Cub Pack opens for a short time.
1963	John Butler, Brian Jones and Allan Roberts go to World Jamboree in Greece.
1964	Decision to reform Deeside Rover Scouts Group.
1964	Gang Show in new HQ.

1965	Welsh Scout Jamboree at Wynnstay Park, Ruabon.
1967	Glyn Barham and David Williams go to Jamboree in Idaho, USA.
1970	Scout Camp, Gilwell Park.
1971	Scout Camp, St.Asaph.
1971	Formation of Second Cub Pack by Christine Roberts & Mrs Ann McFerran.
1972	Scout Camp, Corwen.
1973	Scout Camp, Hanmer.
1974	Scout & Cubs Camp, Tremeirchion.
1975	Scout Camp, Llangollen.
1975	Old Mortuary rented from the council for storage for £1 pcm.
1976	Variety Night held at Kelsterton College.
1976	Fire at H.Q.
1978	Mohawks go to Gilwell.
1978	Scout Camp, Llangollen.
1979	Scout Camp, Gilwell Park.
1979	Venture Scout Group starts.
1979	Train excursion to London.
1980	Extension to HQ.
1980	Scout & Cub Camp, Bala.
1981	Mohawks go to Isle of Man to camp.
1981	Scout Camp, St. Asaph .
1982	Start of Cub football.
1982	Scout Camp, Bala.
1983	Scout Camp, St. Asaph, Pen-y-Bont.
1984	Mohawks go to camp in Dorset.
1985	New Group Badge for neckerchief officially registered.
1986	Beaver Scouts starts.
1986	25th Anniversary celebrations of the opening of the new Scout Hut.
1987	Mohawks go to camp in Scotland.
1987	Bob-a-Job finishes.
1988	Mohawks Camp at Leek.
1990	Mohawk Camp at Monmouth.
1990	Cherokees attend District Camp at Pontins.
1990	Cherokees Camp at Rhydtalog.
1991	Cherokees Camp at Daisy Bank Farm.
1992	Cherokees Sixer/Second Camp at Halkyn.
1992	Cherokees Camp at Tawd Vale.
1992	Cherokees Camp at Tan y Graig.
1993	Cherokees go to London.
1993	Cherokees Sixer/Second Camp at Tan y Graig.
1993	Mohawks at First Aid Competition in Torquay.
1993	Mohawks Camp at Hexham, Northumberland.
1993	Cherokees Camp at Daisy Bank Farm.
1993	Cherokees go to B-P House, London.
1994	Scout Camp, Tawd Vale.
1994	Disabled access fitted to Scout Hut.

1994	Mohawks Camp at Bewdley, Kidderminster.
1994	Cherokees Camp at Tawd Vale.
1994	Cherokees Camp at Tan y Graig.
1994	Mohawks in First Aid Competition at Derby.
1995	Cherokees Camp at Caergwrle.
1995	Cherokees Camp at Queen's Charlotte Wood.
1995	Mohawks at First Aid Competition at Cardiff.
1996–7	Mohawks runners-up in the Hawarden Cup .
1996	Mohawks Camp in Nottingham.
1996	Cherokees Camp at Tawd Vale.
1996	Mohawks at First Aid Competition at Salisbury.
1997	Cherokees Camp at Hadlow Fields.
1997	Cherokees Camp at Rhydtalog.
1998	90th Anniversary Celebration Family Camp at Pontblyddan.
1999	Cherokees Camp at Rhydtalog.
2000	Cherokees Camp at Caergwrle.
2000	Cherokees Camp at Rhydtalog.
2001	Cherokees and Mohawks Camp, Tawd Vale.
2002	Scouts & Cubs Camp, Tawd Vale.
2003	Scouts & Cubs Camp Ashworth Valley, Manchester.
2003	Cherokees Camp at Rhydtalog.
2004	Scouts & Cubs Camp Linnet Clough, Manchester.
2005	Gift Aid Scheme started.
2005	Scouts Camp, Kibblestone.
2005	Cherokees and Mohawks camp at Rhydtalog.
2005	Cherokees & Mohawks Camp,Forest Camp, Sandiway.
2006	Dedication ceremony for Captain Marriott.
2006	Scouts Camp, Kibblestone.
2006	Cherokees and Mohawks Camp, Kibblestone.

Beavers 2007.

3. LISTS

Scout Master/Leaders
E.Ll. Marriott
Harry Butler
Gilbert Butler
John Butler
Neil Summers
Keith Amos
Ray Bewley
Glyn Barham
Allan Roberts

Assistant Scout Masters/Leaders
Graham Allen
Peter Castrey
Robert Conway
Graham Cook
Peter Griffin
Paul Harris
Alan Henshaw
Peter Hutton
Ron Parlane
Len Powell
Shane Rigby
Bryan Roberts
Neil Roberts
Peter Scott
Mr Stretch
Malcolm Turner
Michael Turner
John Williams

Senior Scout Leaders
Tony Lloyd
Harvey Lloyd
John Williams

Venture Scout Leaders
Jeff Howard
Alan Owen
Roy Roberts
Dave Rowlands
John Scott
Frank Wilson

Explorer Scout Leader
Stuart Hicks

Cub Scout Leaders (Akela)
Glyn Bithell
Mike Bowen
Mrs Casey
Tessa Christian
Sue Copp
Pauline Francis
Ken Hart
Brian Jones
Harvey Lloyd
Ian Matthews
Mr Parlane
Ann Roberts
Christine Roberts
Dave Rowlands

Assistant Cub Scout Leaders
Alan Bentley
Gaynor Buckley
Anita Butler
Mr Casey
John Cunningham
Caroline Gilliland
Les Guy
Elaine Hogg
Diane Hollis
Glyn Hopkins
Nora James
Audrey Jones
Brian Jones
Christine Jones
Elaine Jones
Ron Jones
Pauline Leith
Ann McFerran
Andrew Murgatroyd
Andrew Neath
Carrie Prydderch
Shane Rigby
Clive Roberts
Janet Rogers
John Scott

Mark Sephton
Steve Thomas
Harold Weale
Linda Williams
Pat Wilson

Beaver Scout Leaders
Christine Roberts

Assistant Beaver Scout Leaders
Richard Jones
Ron Jones
Stephanie Scott

Group Scout Leaders
E.Ll.Marriott
Harry Butler
Gilbert Butler
Wilson Prydderch
Richard Peers
Roy Christian
Allan Roberts

Scouting Awards

Silver Wolf
Gilbert Butler

Silver Acorn
Gilbert Butler
John Butler
Roy Christian
Allan Roberts

Medals of Merit
E.Ll. Marriott
Harry Butler
Margaret Butler
Gilbert Butler
John Butler
Allan Roberts
Wilson Prydderch
Ian Matthews
Dot Henshaw

King's Scouts
Gilbert Butler
Ken Parlane

Queen's Scouts
Graham Allan
Peter Allan
Glyn Barham
Graham Cook
Garth Dale
Geoffrey Howard
Peter Hutton
Brian Jones
William Kneale
Harvey Lloyd
Allan Roberts
Bryan Roberts
Clive Roberts
David Roberts
Wyn Rowlands
Malcolm Turner
David Williams
John Williams
Graham Hughes
Raymond Wynne

Gilt Cross
Harvey Lloyd
John Williams

Chief Scout Awards
Sean Christian
Graham Cotgreave
Gavin Jones
Michael Gilliland (Bronze)

Long Service Awards
Allan Roberts 40 years
Christine Roberts 25 years
Alan Henshaw 25 years
Ann McFerran 25 years
Neil Roberts 25 years

People who helped build the present Scout H.Q.
Joe Bellis
Fred Brookin
Eddie Coupe
Ken Evans
Freddie Fee
Bill Harrison

Roy Hulley
Edwin Jones
Vaughan Williams
Members of the British
Legion committee in Shotton

**Parents Committee &
Friends of Scouting**
Avril Alexander
Linda Andrews
Ena Baines
Mrs Barham
Denise Bennett
Cath Birtall
Fred Birtall
Hazel Breckon
Mary Brierley
Jane Brown
Ethel Bullock
Margaret Butler
Olwen Butler
Joan Carden
Brian Casey
Ron Cawte
Mrs Cook
Sue Copp
Pauline Cottrell
Chris Cresswell
Collenn Cunningham
Mike Cunnington
Melanie Dandridge
Bridgette Davies
Joan Dixon
Margaret Edward
Betty Evans
Chris Fergusen
Lil Fergusen
Harold Gregory
Lily Gregory
Paul Griffiths
Kate Hart
Dot Henshaw
Gordon Henshaw
Dora Hill
Mona Hogan
Jeff Howard
Joan Howard
Dave Howey
Norma Howey
May Humphries

Peggy Humphries
Joan Jenkins
Alice Jones
Linda Jones
Steven Jones
Trevor Jones
Winston Jones
Gabriella Kiernan
Barbara Knobbes
John Knobbes
Denise Lavery
John Letley
Beattie Lyth
Harry McCormack
Gordan Marshall
Sandra Mellor
Gaynor Morris
Mr Mullett
Joan Oldfield
Sandi Owen
Glenys Peers
Gayle Primrose
Gordan Richards
Bert Rigby
Mrs Rigby
Blodwen Roberts
Bryan Roberts
Eva Roberts
Graham Roberts
Shirley Roberts
Kate Round
Dave Rowlands
Beryl Smallman
Babs Smith
Janet Speed
Jane Styles
Betty Thomas
Craig Thomas
Margaret Thomas
Sheena Thomas
Ron Wallis
Norma Walsh
Harold Weale
John Weale
Alan Williams
Betty Williams
Janet Williams
Pat Wilson
Don Young
Joan Young

Beaver and Cub & Scout Helpers

Denise Bennett
Jackie Bilton
Samantha Butler
Tessa Christian
Beth Copp
Joanne Curtis
Melanie Dandridge
Cathy Evans
Clare Evans
John Evans
Angela Fergusen
Lilian Fergusen
Leanne Gilliland
Harold Gregory
Sue Hansom
Norma Howie
Linda Jones
Ron Jones
Denise Lavery
Michael Lavery
Gaynor Morris
Gail Muia
Catherine O'Donnell
Joan Oldfield
Ellen Pearson
Tracey Peers
Paula Preece
Donna Price
Mrs Saunders
Melanie Smith
Ron Wallis
Harry Weatherhead

Scout Helpers (boys who helped with Cubs and Beavers)

Sam Copp
Michael Dandridge
Michael Gilliland
Zach Hollis
Peter McFerran
Daniel Morris
Terry Owen
Neil Roberts
Richard Roberts
Richard Scott

Sources

Books

Coppack, Tom, *My Life with Ships* (Prescot,1973).

Scout Association, *75 Years of Scouting: a History of the Scout Movement in Word and Pictures* (London, 1982).

Vic Williams, *Connah's Quay: a Civic Century* (Connah's Quay, 1997).

Unpublished Thesis

Bates, Norma, *The Port of Connah's Quay* (Univ. Liverpool, 1980).

Primary Sources

Abstract of Will. Cl. Hurlbutt/Albion Buildings [P/15/1/73].

Buckley, Mold & Deeside Leader, 1950, 1951.

Chester Chronicle, 1903.

Chester Chronicle, 1941, 1942.

Chester Chronicle, 1956, 1957, 1959, 1960, 1962, 1963, 1974,

Chester Chroncle, 1961.

Chester Chronicle, 1965.

Connah's Quay Orders and UDC, 1894/6, FC/C/6/522.

Connah's Quay UDC Minute Book, 1906–08, 1910.

County Herald, 1908.

County Herald, 1919.

Dee Conservancy Board, Part 1& 2, DC/381.

District Council Minute Book, 1901–04, UD/B/1/1.

District Council Minute Book, 1908–15, UD/B/1/4.

Evening School Committee, 1916–17, P/15/1/91.

Flintshire Education Minutes, 1908, FC/2D/8.

Flintshire Education Minutes, 1909, E/MB/15/4.

Flintshire News, March 1910.

Flintshire Observer, 1903.

Flintshire Observer, 1909, 1910, 1911.

Notes to Captain J. Fellowes, NT/1044.

Port of Chester Shipping Register, L/2/G–H S/5.

Records relating to scouting in Flintshire and Clwyd, D/DM/1178/1-25.

Records relating to Welsh scouting, D/KY/1293, 1294, 1296, 1298, 1299, 1302.

St Mark's Church Electoral Roll 1920, P/15/1/19.

St Mark's Church list of communicants, P/15/1/18.

St Mark's Church Minutes, P/15/1/72.